The 1858 Map of Cape Cod, Martha's Vineyard, & Nantucket

by Henry F. Walling
with contributions from
Robert Finch
Theresa Mitchell Barbo
Elliott Carr
Jim Coogan
Charles Fields
Gail Fields
Adam Gamble
Joseph Garver
Kathleen Schatzberg

Co-published
by

Cape Cod's Community Bank® Since 1855

Book design by Adam Gamble, Charles Fields, and Gail Fields.
Editing and production supervision by Adam Gamble.
This book was copy edited by Susan Bouse of Bouse Editorial, Denver, CO.
Photos of Cape Cod Community College's 1858 *Map of the Counties of Barnstable, Dukes and Nantucket, Massachusetts* by Charles Fields.

Printed in South Korea.

10 9 8 7 6 5 4 3 2 1

The following images from the 1858 *Map of the Counties of Barnstable, Dukes and Nantucket, Massachusetts* are reprinted courtesy of the Harvard Map Collection of Harvard Library:

Map Label iii, Provincetown 1858 (Illustration) 1, Steamship (Illustration) 17, The Complete Map 18, Table of Distances 19, Top Portion of the Complete Map 20–21, Bottom Portion of the Complete Map 22–23, Statistics 24, Barnstable County Overview 26, Court House, Barnstable (Illustration) 27, Business Directory for Sandwich 28, Northern Portion of Sandwich (Town) 30–31, Southern Portion of Sandwich (Town) 32–33, Sandwich Village 34, Falmouth (Town) 36, Southern Portion of Falmouth (Town) 38–39, Woods Hole 40, West Falmouth 41, East Falmouth 41, West Barnstable 44, North Sandwich 44, Monument 44, Cotuit Port 44, Northern Portion of Barnstable (Town) 46–47, Southern Portion of Barnstable (Town) 48–49, Centreville 50, Osterville 50, Marston's Mills 50, Brewster (Town) 66–67, Harwich Center 70, South Harwich 71, Chatham Village 74, North Chatham 75, Orleans (Town) 76, Rock Harbor 77, Wellfleet (Village) 80–81, Provincetown (Town) 85, Nomans Land 90, Business Directory for Holmes Hole 90, Business Directory for Edgartown 90, Island of Martha's Vineyard 92-93, Middletown 97, Tisbury (Town) 98, Edgartown (Village) 101, Pacific Bank, Nantucket (Illustration) 103, Central Portion of Nantucket County 106–107, Nantucket (Village) 109, Northern Portion of Nantucket (Village) 110–111, Southern Portion of Nantucket (Village) 112–113, View in Main Street Barnstable (Illustration) 115, Barnstable Bank, Yarmouth Port (Illustration) 119, Harbor of Provincetown, 1620 (Illustration) 122.

The following image from the 1858 *Map of the Counties of Barnstable, Dukes and Nantucket, Massachusetts* is reprinted courtesy of the Norman B. Leventhal Map Center at Boston Public Library: Nantucket County 104–105.

The following images from the 1858 *Map of the Counties of Barnstable, Dukes and Nantucket, Massachusetts* are reprinted courtesy of the William Brewster Nickerson Cape Cod History Archives at Cape Cod Community College:

Geologic Map 25, Sandwich (Town) 28–29, West Sandwich 35, Falmouth (Village) 37, Waquoit 40, North Falmouth 41, Marshpee District 42–43, Barnstable (Town) 45, Hyannis 50–51, Hyannis Port 51, Barnstable Village 52–53, Yarmouth (Town) 54–55, Yarmouth Port and Yarmouth Village 56–57, Dennis (Town) 58–59, Dennis and East Dennis 60–61, South Yarmouth and West Dennis 62, South Dennis and West Harwich 63, East and West Brewster and Brewster Village 64–65, Harwich (Town) 68–69, Harwich Port 71, Chatham (Town) 72–73, Orleans Village 77, Eastham (Town) 78, Wellfleet (Town) 79, Truro (Town) 82–83, Truro Village 83, Provincetown Village 84, Business Directory for Provincetown 84, Pond Village 84, Top Portion of Provincetown Village 86–87, Top Portion of Business Directory for Provincetown 86–87, Bottom Portion of Provincetown Village 88–89, Bottom Portion of Business Directory for Provincetown 88–89, Pond Village 89, Sailing Ship (Illustration) 91, Elizabeth Islands 94–95, West Tisbury 96, Gay Head (Town) 96, Chilmark (Town) 96–97, Holmes' Hole 99, Edgartown (Town) 100, Muskegat Channel 102, Siasconset 108, Business Directory for Nantucket 114.

MANUFACTURERS.

ARTICLES PRODUCED.		ANNUAL VALUE PRODUCED.	
	Barnstable.	Dukes.	Nantucket.
Woollen Goods	$ 23000	$ 3400	$
Wrought Iron	24700		12000
Cast	30000		
Machinery	10000		
Tacks & Brads	20000		
Glass	600000		
Boots	1168	1536	3068
Shipping	147724	11850	20912
Salt	236176	31	
Carriages	11420		
Sperm Candles, Oil &c.	10200	468855	788104
Tin Ware	9800	200	4000
Leather	11900	2500	
Boots & Shoes	18240	1068	10276

FISHERIES.

	Barnstable.	Dukes.	Nantucket.
Sperm & Whale Oil & Bone	$ 196963	$ 49350	$ 420870
Mackerel & Cod	806366		4238
Alewive, Shad & Salmon	11258	3000	700
Total Value Produced	309242	762232	1608800

POPULATION.

Barnstable County.		
Barnstable	4996	
Brewster	1525	Wellfleet ... 2325
Chatham	2560	Yarmouth ... 2592
Dennis	3497	Total ... 35872
Eastham	808	Dukes County.
Falmouth	2613	Chilmark ... 667
Harwich	3261	Edgartown ... 1898
Orleans	1754	Tisbury ... 1827
Provincetown	3096	Total ... 4407
Sandwich	4495	Nantucket County.
Truro	1917	Nantucket ... 8800

PROVINCETOWN 1858.

CAPE COD HARBOR

PROVINCETOWN VILLAGE

CAPE COD HARBOR

Long Point Light

House Point Island

Lobster Plain

MAP

OF THE COUNTIES OF

BARNSTABLE, DUKES AND NANTUCKET

Massachusetts.

Based upon the trigonometrical Survey of the State, the Details from Actual Surveys under the Direction of

HENRY F. WALLING

SUPᵗ OF THE STATE MAP.

1858.

Engraved, Printed, Colored & Mounted at

H. F. WALLINGS

MAP ESTABLISHMENT

Nº 90 Fulton St. NEW YORK.

PUBLISHED BY

D. R. SMITH & CO.

106 WASHINGTON Sᵗ. BOSTON

AND

90 FULTON Sᵗ. NEW YORK.

A large portion of the Coast is laid down from materials obtained from the archives of the U.S. COAST SURVEY

PROVINCETOWN VILLAGE

Scale 1/8000

TRURO VILLAGE

Scale 1/8000

Mill Pond

Billingsgate

BUSINESS DIRECTORY

BANKS.

Provincetown Bank, S. Freeman Prest. Eliph. Smith Cashr. Commercial St.
Seamans Savings Bank, B.E. Nickerson Prest Union Exchange

INSURANCE OFFICES.

Atlantic Mutual Insurance Co. B.E. Nickerson Jun. Surry Union Exch.
Equitable Marine N.B. Freeman, Surry Commercial St.

SHIP STORES.

Union Wharf Co.	Commercial Street
E.S. Smith & Co.	Central Wharf
J.E. & G. Bowley	Bowley's Wharf
Paine Nickerson & Co.	Union Exchange
T. & J.H. Hilliard & Co.	Commercial Wharf
Freeman & Chapman	Commercial Street
Paine & Emery	
Daniel Small	
E. & B.E. Cook	
S. Cook Jun.	
D. Conwell	
Nickerson & Tuck	City Wharf
H. & S. Cook & Co.	Eastern Packet Pier.

DRY GOODS DEALERS.

Charles Nickerson ... Commercial Street
Rufus Conant Jun.

CLOTHING DEALERS.

J.F. Small ... Commercial Street
W. Boyne

MILLINERY & FANCY GOODS.

Godfrey Ryder Jun. ... Commercial Street
Ann Nickerson
Mrs. S.A. Paine

VARIETY STORES.

H. Willard ... Commercial Street

FURNITURE DEALERS.

Baker & Sellew, Cooks Block Commercial Street

JEWELLERS.

Dudley & Long ... Commercial Street

DENTISTS.

Dr. A.S. Dudley ... Commercial Street

SAIL MAKERS.

C.A. Hannum	Union Wharf
F.A. Paine	Central Wharf
Paul Atkins	Commercial Street
C.D. Cook	
S. Bangs Jun. Bangs Whf.	
C.H. Dyer	
Parker Pettis	Market Wharf

ROCK HARBOR

iii

Dedication

Dedicated to
Mary Sicchio and Charlotte Schuster Price
for their years of exemplary service as archivists at the
William Brewster Nickerson Cape Cod History Room at Cape Cod Community College.

Charlotte Schuster Price served as the first archivist from 1978 until 1993.
Mary Sicchio has served as the second archivist since 1993.
Together they have enriched the lives of countless students of this beloved region's history.

Contents

Contents

Illustrations

Tables and Business Directories

Editor's Preface

Adam Gamble

The 1858 *Map of the Counties of Barnstable, Dukes and Nantucket, Massachusetts* by Henry F. Walling, was created for display on the walls of prominent businesses, government offices, private studies, and civic institutions. Transforming such a document into book form is no simple task. One might just as soon try to put the beaches of the Cape Cod National Seashore, Chappaquiddick Island, or Siasconset in book form.

Of course, there have been plenty of "optimists" who have tried to do just that—put these precious places into a book. Henry David Thoreau visited the area in 1849, 1850, 1855, and in 1857. Thoreau's book *Cape Cod* was published in 1864, and in the years since, there has been a myriad of writers, artists, and photographers who have published their own books about this region. In some cases, these creative people have indeed managed to capture, in book form, a certain "essence" of the original. But no matter how great their spirit or adept their skills, their books ultimately amount to a "translation"—often wonderful, but always distinctly different from the original.

So, as the editor of this book, I might as well come out and say it here: This map was never intended to be published in book form! Those interested in studying the map might just as fruitfully do so by going to the website of the Norman B. Leventhal Map Center at Boston Public Library (http://maps.bpl.org/), where one can examine the 1858 map, and many others, with amazing fluidity from an internet browser anywhere in the world. Alternatively, one might visit one of the original wall maps still displayed in a public place: in the William Brewster Nickerson Cape Cod History Archives at Cape Cod Community College, in the lobby of the Cape Cod Five bank operations center in Orleans, or at various libraries and historical repositories around the region.

So, why publish this book? The most obvious answer is to create a community project that raises both awareness and funds for the William Brewster Nickerson Cape Cod History Archives at Cape Cod Community College. The archives are one of our region's great treasure troves, and they deserve our support.

Perhaps even more important than supporting the archives, however, is that there does seem to be a genuine, inherent value in "converting" this map into a book. Reissuing it at its original five-foot-by-five-foot size would not be a practical format for most people to own or to display—although that could be a worthwhile future project. But, even if the map were republished at its original size, as a wall map, the writing at that size remains extremely small and difficult to read, even more difficult than you'll find it in this book. Be forewarned that if you go to view one of the originals, you should bring a magnifying glass—and be prepared to crouch down to see the lower portions and perhaps to stand on tiptoes to view the upper portions.

As for the option of viewing the map through a computer screen or digital device, it must be said that even with the continuing advances in technology, there still remains something wonderfully "user friendly" about books, about the process of flipping from page to page with one's fingers and thumbs—with no unsightly power cords, and no batteries necessary, just the smells of ink and paper.

Publishing the map in book form provides a medium wherein many individual town maps (and most of the larger village maps) can be presented on their own pages or page spreads. Placing smaller portions of the map on individual pages also has allowed most of them to be magnified significantly, so they are at least a little easier to read than on the original, although you will likely still find benefit in the use of a magnifying glass. In addition, it is hoped that the physical attributes of this book—produced in a luxurious display format with one-foot-by-one-foot pages—convey at least some sense of the grandeur of the original.

Books also continue to be excellent mediums for packaging related materials together, "under one cover." In this case, we were able to include essays from a number of thoughtful writers and scholars, each of whom kindly donated their work to help support the archives. Publishing the map in book form has also allowed the use of images from three different originals: from Cape Cod Community College, from the Norman B. Leventhal Map Center at Boston Public Library, and from the Harvard Map Collection of the Harvard Library. As we do not know of an original 1858 map that is still in pristine condition—free from all rips and tears, repair marks, water stains, pencil markings, cracked paper, etc.—it worked well to combine images from multiple sources. For each page in this book, pains were taken to choose between all three options. The result, we hope, is a sense of the 1858 map as a historical object in and of itself.

Interestingly, the Cape Cod Community College map has two map insets featured on it that are not printed on either the Harvard or Boston Public Library maps. The map insets for the villages of Dennis and East Dennis and of Harwich Port simply do not exist on the Harvard and Boston Public Library originals. Dr. Joseph Garver, the reference librarian of the Harvard Map Collection, confirms that it was common practice in the nineteenth century for mapmakers to add details to succeeding print runs, especially if a map was popular or in demand, or if the mapmaker thought the additions would improve

sales. By not limiting our book to one original source, we were able to easily include all the insets.

One major issue in converting the wall map to book form was that of organization. This book includes 132 bound pages, plus a cover and a book jacket, whereas the original map was a single flat surface.

Starting with a map of the region as a continuous whole, the original mapmakers overlaid the major bodies of saltwater with the map insets, illustrations, and other items. The map insets of the various towns and villages were necessary, because even at the approximate five-foot-by-five-foot size, there was simply not enough room in the more densely populated areas to include the names of the heads of households or the businesses that coincide with each black dot representing each building on the regional map. These map insets are essentially "close-ups" of each village and town. They are the nineteenth-century equivalent of "zooming in" by clicking the plus button on a digital map.

The mapmakers also wanted to include valuable demographic and industry statistics, business listings, as well as the Table of Distances and the Geologic Map. This information increased the value of the original maps, helping to sell more of them. The business listings were also an important source of income for the mapmakers, as each business paid to be listed.

Some of the illustrations on the map were included, not only as adornments to the maps, but as regional symbols, such as "Harbor of Provincetown, 1620," the year the *Mayflower* dropped anchor there. Others, such as the illustration of the Barnstable Bank in Yarmouth Port, which is no longer in business, were paid for by subscription. Similarly, we are proud today to have Cape Cod Five, the largest locally based bank on the Cape, co-publish this book to support our area's heritage and the history archives at Cape Cod Community College. Cape Cod Five was founded in 1855, just three years before this map was published, the same year of the state census that is used for the map's Table of Statistics.

When Henry F. Walling and his team put the different aspects of the 1858 map together, it seems they were guided as much by "organic" concerns of size and shape as by any overriding logic. Certainly, there is a sense that related items ought to be grouped together, such as placing the business directory for Nantucket adjacent to the map of the village of Nantucket. They also sensibly placed the business directory and the village inset in the general vicinity of the map of Nantucket County, in the bottom right quadrant. But, in some cases, the placement of items seems more random. For example, the placement of the map label directly under Provincetown Harbor doesn't seem especially ideal. Shouldn't the label be in a more central position? Perhaps at the top and center of the map? And does the map inset for North Chatham really belong below the island of Martha's Vineyard? Similarly, why is the inset map for the village of East and West Brewster placed so far west of Sandwich, way over next to Wareham? The mapmakers were ultimately as influenced by the dictates of the shape and size of each village as they were by any system of proximity or of social prominence. The fact is that no matter how hard they tried, there simply wasn't enough room to put each village inset map in the immediate proximity to that village's location on the regional map. They seemed to have rightly concluded that neither geographic landmasses nor the human settlements on them fit easily into uniform boxes and shapes. As a result, the 1858 map has a certain jigsaw puzzle feel to it that is at once a little disorienting but also generally pleasing and even satisfying to view.

In organizing these items—the maps, illustrations, and other elements—into book form, we tried to group them in as coherent a manner as possible while trying to remain true to the original document. While focusing on readability, we too have had to let the "organic" nature of the region's geography and community take precedence. Thus, the book is divided into seven sections: Commentary, The Complete Map and General Items, Barnstable County, Dukes County, Nantucket County, Contributors and Acknowledgments, and Index. Having seven sections allows each to start with one of the eight illustrations featured on the original wall map, and then to conclude the book with the illustration of Provincetown Harbor in 1620. And if one thinks of the front matter of this book (title page, copyright page, dedication, table of contents, and this preface) as a section, then the map label can be thought of as that section's illustration.

The Complete Map and General Items section starts with a single-page illustration of the whole map. It also includes two sets of page spreads, one showing the northern portion of the map, the other the southern portion, so readers can get an idea of the map as a whole. This section also includes the Geologic Map, the Table of Distances, and the Statistics.

Next, the three county sections are presented in alphabetical order: Barnstable, Dukes, and Nantucket. Each county section starts with overviews of that county. It then proceeds to show each township within the county grouped, as closely as possible, with the various villages within that township.

In the case of Barnstable County, the towns are presented in a general order from west to east, as if one were traveling from the mainland to Provincetown, visiting each town along the way. Thus, it shows the Town of Sandwich and its village insets, the Town of Falmouth and its village insets, "Marshpee District" (for which the wall map doesn't have any village insets), the Town of Barnstable with its village insets, and so on to Provincetown. Because of the differing sizes of the maps on the original, it is not always possible for us to start each town section with the complete town map, although we have tried to do so wherever possible. There is also the issue of the original mapmakers creating map insets that include villages from two different towns, such as the map inset of the villages of South Yarmouth and West Dennis combined on one map. In such cases, we do not repeat the map in both town sections. There are also some groupings of small map insets of villages on the original wall map that have been kept together. And there are some pages in this book onto which we have grouped small map insets. Giving each of these small village inset maps individual pages would simply be awkward and unnecessary, as they can only be enlarged so far before they become distorted and more difficult to read. This also means that in a few instances village inset maps are grouped with village inset maps from other towns. This is how they appear on the original wall map.

In the case of Dukes County, a general west-to-east presentation of the towns is followed. In the case of Nantucket County, the island, which is itself both a county and a township, is presented as a whole, followed by a close-up of the center of the island, then by the village insets and the business directory. The book concludes with the Contributors and Acknowledgments section and an Index section.

Readers will notice that in organizing these maps, we often include the details from the original map that surround an individual town, village or other item. The photographer and book publisher, Charles Fields, who volunteered to photograph the Cape Cod Community College map for this project, first proposed this presentation. It allows viewers to not only focus on the individual map or map groupings featured on each page at an enlarged size but in many cases to get a sense of how that map or map grouping was incorporated into the complete wall map design. Descriptive headers and footers have been omitted from the map pages because this would distract from the original image. This also avoids redundancy, since labels were already included on the originals from 1858. Page numbers are included in the bottom outside corners of most pages to facilitate locating items via the table of contents and index, but page numbers are omitted where they might interfere with information on the page.

The result is a physical object that is very different from the original wall map on which it is based. Again, these maps were not made with any plans for their being printed in a book with twelve-inch-by-twelve-inch pages. They were created two years before Abraham Lincoln was elected president, three years before the American Civil War began. The wall map was published at a time when windmills and whaling, salt making and steamships were prominent throughout the region. In contrast, the book you are now reading was printed in the early years of the twenty-first century. This book is actually going to press at a time when US President Barack Obama and his family are vacationing on Martha's Vineyard, a fact that speaks volumes both about our time and about our place. This is also a time when American soldiers, including Cape Codders and Islanders, are fighting in Iraq and Afghanistan. Terrorism is a major concern, and the world is in a deep recession. Wind turbines are proposed for Nantucket Sound, and digital technology is rapidly transforming our world, including turning the publishing world upside down. Who can imagine what people will think of this book a century and a half from now, in 2158?

We can only hope this twenty-first-century "translation" of this nineteenth-century wall map is able to capture some of the essence of the original. It truly does represent the "olde" Cape Cod, Martha's Vineyard, and Nantucket of our dreams and imaginations. The important question, of course, is how we each incorporate the many insights offered by it into our present realities, and thus into our dreams and imaginations for the future of Cape Cod, Martha's Vineyard, and Nantucket.

Commentary

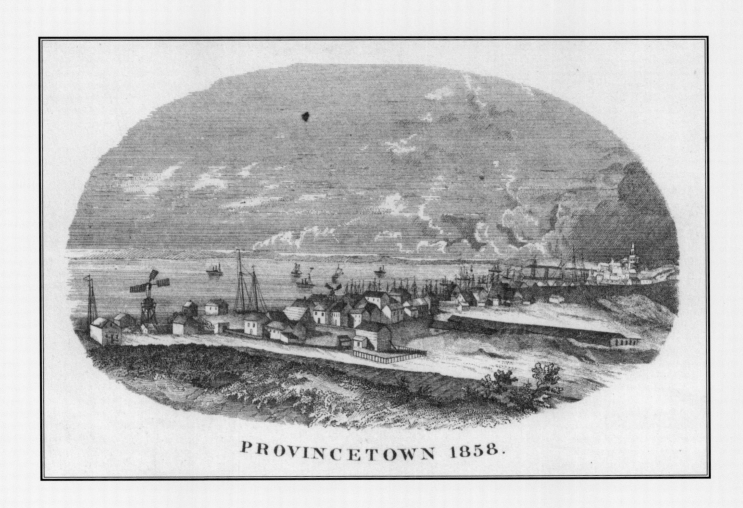

PROVINCETOWN 1858.

Our Stories, Ourselves: Preserving Our Heritage for Generations to Come

Kathleen Schatzberg, President of Cape Cod Community College

It is said that those who forget their history are doomed to repeat it. It is a dour warning, to be sure, and one that takes a deep nod to unsavory aspects of our shared history. But there's a flip side to that coin: Those who forget history are deprived of the celebration of past achievements that can illuminate and enrich our shared future.

Even as today's world gets closer to accepting "virtual reality" as an acceptable alternative to really "being there," archeologists, historians, and treasure hunters continue to search for the "real thing," the artifact itself—the source from which the legends and stories of a people were fashioned as a means of preserving a culture's most prized possession: its essence, its history. And, history is a profoundly powerful teacher. As the well-known saying proclaims, history's lessons are ignored at our peril and impoverishment. For these very reasons, over the centuries, conquerors almost always sought to destroy the repositories of history, the great libraries, and the artifacts of a conquered people, for once the sources of a culture's heritage were destroyed, a new reality could be fashioned with relative ease.

Even without human mayhem, our memories are fragile: They fade over time, become subject to embellishment as well as degradation, and generally become unreliable without some technological means of preservation. This has been the genius of humanity, beginning with the written word and going on to books and artifacts, preserving the history that our human brains inevitably lose, even in one lifetime, let alone over centuries. Thus, preserving the sources of our history is a prime responsibility, enabling us and generations to come to know our own history, to celebrate it, and to avoid the mistakes of those who preceded us.

The William Brewster Nickerson Cape Cod History Archives at Cape Cod Community College represents that commitment to preserving our history. The same commitment today drives its expansion. Over the college's nearly fifty-year history, these treasured archives have become the center of new knowledge and of its dissemination, and the repository of priceless records and artifacts that hold the essence of this region, the writings, images, and creations of its people.

A crucially important effort is underway to aid in the archives' preservation and expand the public's access to its historic holdings that illuminate seventeenth-, eighteenth-, and nineteenth-century life during times when Cape Cod people lived far more simply, primarily off the land and sea, while also becoming an integral part of forging a young democracy. These early European generations learned from the native people here a deep respect and appreciation for this tiny slip of land jutting into the sea, an appreciation that has been passed on to each succeeding generation. The histories of these two peoples—natives and new arrivals—became inextricably intertwined, and it now falls to us to keep passing along this shared history to the generations yet to come.

Cape Cod Community College has embraced its fragile home and works tirelessly to preserve and sustain both the environment and the history of the people who depend on it so deeply. The effort to expand the William Brewster Nickerson Cape Cod History Archives is a vital part of that commitment because in preserving our heritage and providing open access to its artifacts, we pass on the core values that sustain us all, even as we deal with each day's enormous challenges.

The college's mission statement ends with a fitting summary that applies particularly well to the expansion project now underway: "We honor our past, celebrate our present, and imagine the future." The preservation and enhancement of the Nickerson Archives is a core means of fulfilling that mission.

The publication of this book is a major part of that effort. Through its printing and purchase, it becomes an extension of the Nickerson archival legacy, bringing directly into schools, libraries, and homes some snapshots of Cape Cod life at mid-nineteenth century, a fascinating glimpse of our shared history before electricity, before the automobile, before the economy moved from fishing and farming to development and tourism.

Readers who explore the past as preserved here in this exceptional atlas—an enlightening and engaging look into life on Cape Cod in and around 1858—will also, I hope, choose to honor our past by joining in the Nickerson Archives preservation effort. Visit the archives on our campus; celebrate and share in the outstanding education opportunities offered every day; and take the time to imagine what the future would be like without the repositories of knowledge, history, and culture like

those of these treasured archives that we hold in trust for everyone who can learn from it now and for future generations. How empty would be our lives in today's "virtual world" without the preservation of these primary sources?

Enjoy the atlas, come visit the William Brewster Nickerson Cape Cod History Archives, and help us fulfill our responsibility to the future.

Two Windows

Robert Finch

There I had got the Cape under me, as much as if I were riding it bare-backed. It was not as on the map, or seen from the stage-coach; but there I found it all out of doors, huge and real, Cape Cod! as it cannot be represented on a map, color it as you will; the thing itself, than which there is nothing more like it, no truer picture or account, which you cannot go further and see.
—Henry David Thoreau, *Cape Cod* (1864)

Thoreau's explosion of hyperbolic elation comes at the moment of finally reaching Cape Cod's Great Beach in 1848, after a long and often uncomfortable journey from Sandwich to Orleans in a stagecoach over the Cape's sandy, rutted roads. It can be read as, among other things, an implied reprimand to those who prefer looking at maps or other secondhand representations of a place to experiencing "the thing itself" firsthand. But the absolute pronouncements of Concord's native son often covered up their opposites. Just as Thoreau's celebration of solitude in *Walden* carefully omitted his regular weekend trips back home for a home-cooked meal, so we should note that Thoreau did not alight on Cape Cod with innocent eyes. Not only had he read everything he could find on the subject before coming to the Cape, he also had traced a copy of an earlier map of Cape Cod that he consulted in detail and very likely brought with him to orient himself on his travels. Moreover, he often made his own maps of places he traveled to, near and far, for despite his cosmic outlook and transcendental sensibilities, he liked to get his factual details right.

Maps are artifacts of their time, and, as such, they are windows, not only on the world of the past that they represent, but on the worldview or the mind of the time that produced them. For instance, we like to think that our own maps have grown increasingly accurate and objective with advances in surveying techniques and satellite photography, but they are as much objects of convention and culture as those of the distant past. On global maps, the Northern Hemisphere still holds sway, representing the world with ourselves at the top, and our two-dimensional world maps still choose to put the United States in the center, leaving Russia, the largest country in the world, to tear itself in two for the convenience of our Americocentrism.

Just so, the 1858 map of Cape Cod, Nantucket, and Martha's Vineyard reproduced in this book gives us both a wide-angle or macroview of its time, and, if we look at it closely and read between the lines, a more intimate or microview of the age that made it and the people it represents. Within its carefully drawn and shaded boundaries and formal lists and tables, it seethes with human stories and human meaning.

The 1858 map is hardly the first of its kind, as the earliest known approximations of parts of the Cape and Islands were rendered over 250 years earlier by Bartholomew Gosnold and Samuel de Champlain. Moreover, although it claims to be based on a "trigonometrical Survey of the State," it is not, strictly speaking, a "geological survey" map. Although the actual landmass outlines and town borders are fairly accurate, the locations of streets, ponds, and some geological features are often approximate or selective. There are no true contour lines; instead, a few prominent hills are represented without elevations and with dramatic sunburst cartographical design, suggesting a loftiness greater than they actually possess. So all maps represent selectively, highlighting what their makers deem useful and significant.

Any map represents a moment in time, and the 1858 map represents an especially significant one for the Cape and Islands. As Jim Coogan points out in detail in his essay, it was the high-water mark of the Cape's maritime prosperity, represented by the abundance of shipyards, wharves, and the number of maritime businesses listed for the major harbors. But the contemporary viewer is also struck by the momentariness of that moment. That is, we look at this map and see numerous changes that were to come in the presence of land forms and communities now vanished: Wellfleet's Billingsgate Island, Provincetown's Long Point settlement, the "inland waterway" connecting Nauset Harbor with Pleasant Bay in Orleans, and the break at "Old Harbor" on Chatham's North Beach (which reminds us that the present break, created by the storm of 1987, is part of a cyclical pattern of that dynamic beach system), among others.

Other changes to come are apparent by their absence on the map: the town of Bourne, carved out of Sandwich in 1884; the extension of the Cape Cod Railroad to Provincetown in 1873; the Cape Cod Canal, finally completed in 1914; the creation of the Mid-Cape Highway in the 1950s; the establishment of the Cape Cod National Seashore in 1961; and, of course, the explosion of new development and transportation facilities after World War II that transformed the Cape and Islands from rural backwaters to suburban communities and national vacation destinations.

Less visually discernable on the map, but looming in the historian's mind, is the shadow of the Civil War, which would come only three years after the map's publication and forever change the face of all America. The war, however, would also prove a disaster for the Cape and Islands' shipping industry and marked the beginning of a long economic decline from which it did not really recover until another major war eighty years later.

But 1858 was also a moment of major transition in technology that would have taken place with or without the war. There are, for instance, a number of "saltworks" still represented. Salt-making by evaporation of seawater was a major industry on Cape Cod in the first half of the nineteenth century, but the discovery of salt mines in the West in the 1840s had already reduced the number of saltworks to a mere fraction of what it was in its heyday. We also see a few other older industries hanging on—grist mills, windmills, and clipper shipyards—representing technologies that would soon become obsolete as steam, steel, and electricity replaced wind, water, and wood. In 1858, Nantucket and Edgartown, which built their prosperity on whales, still show surprisingly sizeable incomes from the production of "Sperm Candles, Oil, etc.," but the following year, the first petroleum well in the United States would be drilled in Titusville, Pennsylvania, dooming the domestic whaling industry.

Some of these social, economic, and cultural changes to come are already incipient on this map. Two of its novel features are the detailed insets of the major towns and villages, and the statistics listing population, distances, and the value of local agriculture, fishing, and industries. The first indicates the growing importance of the towns as centers of community life, and the second the growth in the capital assessment of society. In other words, by 1858, the business of Cape Cod was business, and increasingly it was concentrated in the towns, now becoming connected to the outside world by rail.

There is even a hint of the scientific revolution that was taking place at the time this map was made. Geology as a modern science was only a few decades old, but in the lower left-hand corner we find a small inset of a "Geological Map" of the three counties, compiled by Edward Hitchcock, the first State Geologist of Massachusetts. Hitchcock was a very astute and discerning scientist, but his map does not yet reflect the revolutionary theories of glaciation by Harvard's Louis Agassiz, which within a few years would forever change our geological view of the formation of the Cape Cod and the Islands.

So the map before us is rich in historical and geographical information, and, from our contemporary perspective, fraught with changes to come, both human and natural. But beyond the macroview—the layouts of roads and villages, the geological and geographical features, the identification of householders, the economic and technological statistics—what kind of a microview does the map give us? What can it tell us about the character, sensibilities, and daily life of the people of Cape Cod and the Islands at that moment in time?

These questions involve a more subjective viewing, but for me, one telling feature is that, unlike contemporary maps, the individual townships of the Cape and Islands are shaded in different colors, suggesting a strong and even passionate identification with particular communities, a kind of local xenophobia whose remnants we still cling to today and which still dog us at town meetings in our attempts to deal with regional issues on a local basis.

Also, unlike modern highway maps, almost no distinctions are made between major and minor roads. They spread out from the villages like a web of identical capillaries rather than the hierarchical system of main arteries, secondary highways, and local streets that we are used to today. One of the frustrating pleasures this map affords is trying to identify existing roads today with their representations on this map. Some roads that are now obscure dirt lanes that seem to go from nowhere to nowhere were, in 1858, major thoroughfares for traveling from one village to another. All roads were unpaved, most were unnamed, and travel was slower and more democratic.

Or take the "Business Directories" that are shown for some of the more prominent communities. From the number of maritime-related businesses and firms listed for Provincetown, one could make the case that it was the most prosperous and commercial town at the time. But its future as a major tourist destination also seems suggested in the listings of three doctors, two hotels and one "saloon," a dentist, a furniture dealer, a jeweler, and three "Millinery and Fancy Goods" stores. On the other hand, Nantucket, Provincetown's commercial rival, may not have possessed as many "fashionable" stores as the Cape Tip, but it appears it could lay claim to a more

educated, sophisticated, and perhaps more litigious populace, since it boasted no fewer than four lawyers, four "Libraries and Reading Rooms," and even an "E. Mitchell Books" on Main Street, which, by remarkable coincidence, has nearly the same name as Mitchell's Book Store on Nantucket's Main Street today, though there is apparently no relation between them.

Occasionally, a feature on the map may resonate with one's own personal history here. Take, for instance, the small triangles that mark some of the hill summits that are selectively represented. These triangles indicate "signals," which one might assume meant navigational beacons. One of these marked summits, located in West Brewster, where I lived for many years, is in fact labeled "Signal Hill." I once discovered an old, rotting, wooden flagpole at the top of this hill and was told by the owner of the property that its name came from the fact that it was used to signal the local populace when a packet-mail boat from Boston was arriving by the rather curious expedient of raising a wooden barrel up the pole. In later years, long after the packets had disappeared, the same pole was used to indicate when neighborhood dances were held on Saturday nights.

One of the most valuable features of this map is that it shows, for the first time, not only every residence on the Cape and Islands, but the name of each and every head-of-household, inked in elegant script next to the small, black squares representing houses. This has great value to historians, genealogists, and real estate–title researchers, but, on a more human level, it also speaks to an endearing sense of social stability, the feeling that one belonged, not only to a town or a village within that town, but to a particular house within that village and town— that one's place in the world was set, if not in stone, then at least in ink. This must have been reassuring in an age where one's hold on life was much more tenuous than today (although perhaps it speaks to us more directly now that our hold on our own domiciles has been shaken by the recent collapse of the housing market).

Some of these century-and-a-half-old names may strike the viewer as familiar. On the Wellfleet map, for instance, on the east side of Swett's Pond, there are three residences belonging to Newcombs. One of these is the house of John Newcomb, the "Wellfleet Oyster-man" whom Thoreau memorialized in his book in one of the most deadpan, hilarious passages he ever wrote. Swett's Pond is now called Williams Pond, reminding us also that local names were not as permanent or official as they are now. One particularly interesting name change is that of Long Pond in Truro, which at some point had its name changed to Horseleech Pond. I can't help wondering what led to the change. Is it possible that, as the summer population grew, the locals decided to rebaptize the pond with such a deliberately uninviting name to discourage "outsiders" from using it?

Occasionally, the names on the map suggest a darker story. Along with the names of the male heads-of-households, one finds an occasional "Mrs. Dyer" or "Mrs. Small," a convention of the time that usually denoted the status of a widow. These are relatively few in number, except when one looks at the inset map for Truro Village. In this relatively small circumference, there are no less than seventeen "Mrs.'s." The explanation lies in the tragic gale of October 3, 1841, in which the lives of fifty-seven Truro men were lost at sea. So moved was Thoreau when he learned of this event that he wrote one of the most compressed expressions of domestic loss in American literature: "Who lives in that house," I inquired. "Three widows," was the reply. Seventeen years after the gale, Truro Center was still a village of widows.

Danger and death at sea were, of course, part of the daily life of local residents in 1858, as represented by the number of "Humane Houses" and "Life Boats" marked along the Cape and Islands' remote beaches. The name "Humane House" was grander than the reality, for these were a series of crude shacks erected in the late 1700s by the Massachusetts Humane Society into which a shipwrecked sailor might crawl and shiver in the hopes that someone would find him before he froze or starved to death. Sometimes these huts were furnished with blankets, dried food, matches, and firewood, but when Thoreau came upon one of these Humane Houses or "Charity Houses" on the outer beach, he found only

"some stones and some loose wads of wool on the floor, and an empty fireplace at the further end," and he concluded, "how cold is charity! How inhumane humanity!" With the establishment of the U.S. Life Saving Service in 1872, these crude Humane Houses were replaced by a series of manned stations that stretched from Race Point in Provincetown to Chatham.

Still, there is at least one juxtaposition on this map that reflects an ambivalence of attitude toward sea disasters that we find difficult to comprehend today. On the Provincetown map, on the ocean side of the dunes, a "Life Boat" sits next to "Stone and Mayo's Wreck House." The "Life Boats" were also supplied by the Humane Society and presumably were manned by local volunteers. The "Wreck House" represents a major business on Cape Cod throughout the nineteenth century, namely "wrecking" or salvaging the cargo of the hundreds of shipwrecks that foundered on the outer bars of Cape Cod. The proximity of the two illustrates the mixed reactions the local populace often experienced simultaneously toward such wrecks: On one hand they represented personal tragedies, often spurring heroic efforts to save a ship's crew; on the other, they were economic windfalls, to be exploited as best they could.

By making available the 1858 *Map of the Counties of Barnstable, Dukes and Nantucket, Massachusetts* the Cape Cod Five and On Cape Publications offer the viewer two windows on the past as well as perhaps providing a perspective on our own time. In its graphic representations, statistics, directories, and individual names, we can find both an informative and revealing history of the times and fascinating glimpses into the lives and attitudes of the people who inhabited its real-world space. In doing so, we may also be spurred to contemplate our own contemporary forms of cartographical representation and orientation—the risk-encouraging personal GPS systems; the narrow, blinkered abstractions of MapQuest; the voyeuristic appeal of Google Earth—and ask what they tell us about our own moment in time, the way we see, experience, and think about our own life maps.

The Cartographer: Henry F. Walling

Joseph Garver

In the nineteenth century, most American cartographers earned their daily bread serving the needs of local clients–platting real estate parcels, surveying roads, mapping town boundaries, or charting the inland and coastal waters within their own community and its immediate neighbors. Other cartographers, by inclination or necessity, courted a regional or national audience for their works. As his career developed, Henry Francis Walling (1825–1888) increasingly belonged to the latter category of mapmaker. Born in Burrillville, Rhode Island, and educated in Providence, he ultimately made his mark far beyond his native state. In the midst of all of his projects, however, he managed to take a particularly active role in the mapping of New England.

After serving his apprenticeship as a protégé of Samuel B. Cushing, a prominent Providence surveyor, Walling set up his own mapmaking business around 1850–first in Boston, then in New York City. Over the next three decades, his company produced hundreds of town plans and county maps, nearly twenty state maps and atlases, and a variety of specialized cartographic products, including steamboat and railroad guides. However, Walling was most active in Massachusetts, where he mapped nearly fifty communities and all of the fourteen counties.

Walling built upon solid cartographic foundations in Massachusetts. From the colonial period onward, the state was at the forefront of efforts to chart its coast and survey its terrain. In 1794 and again in 1830, the state legislature required each town to submit a manuscript survey of its roads, waterways, boundaries, industries, and public buildings. These submissions served as the basis for Carleton Osgood (in several editions after 1798) and Simeon Borden (in 1844) to compile their official maps of Massachusetts. In recognition of his surveying capabilities and his publication experience, the Massachusetts legislature appointed Walling superintendent of the state map in 1855. While updating Simeon Border's 1844 map of Massachusetts, Walling assembled the most accurate data from a variety of sources, including the U.S. Coast Survey, before publishing his county maps and, eventually, his Official Topographical Atlas of Massachusetts (1871). Shortly before his death, he also served as coordinator of federal-state activities in producing the first topographical survey of Massachusetts.

Walling's 1858 *Map of the Counties of Barnstable, Dukes and Nantucket, Massachusetts* is typical of the county maps that he produced during his career–comprehensive in scope, encyclopedic in range, highly decorative, and dense with information about topographical features, local industries, public institutions, and landowners. In the process of producing hundreds of these wall maps, Walling and his associates devised a streamlined method of compiling the surveys and collecting ancillary information such as property ownership. While surveying teams employed compasses and odometers to measure the length and trajectory of roads, other researchers would simultaneously assemble data from town records and other printed sources.

Because these maps were sold by subscription, Walling and his competitors embellished their publications with features that not only satisfied the utilitarian function of orientation but also responded to less-tangible needs. The attractive graphics delighted the eye; the identification of property holders appealed to pride in ownership; and the inclusion of topographical detail answered a basic human urge to see how people and their works fit into the natural environment. These maps were designed for display in the parlors, businesses, schools, and public offices of the communities depicted in them, so publishers strove to enhance their marketability with vignettes of local landmarks, business directories, and insets providing detailed information about major population centers.

Maps of that era continue to serve us today, offering us invaluable insights into the economic and social life of the Cape and Islands in the mid-nineteenth century. Walling's 1858 map shows this region when it was still actively engaged in maritime activities. The detailed descriptions of businesses along the streets of these towns—with their sail lofts, ship carpenters, spar makers, saltworks, oil sheds, candle manufactories, boatyards, and wharves—conjure up a time when the inhabitants of these coastal communities were intimately attuned to the winds and tides. In fact, many of them claimed, with some justice, that they knew the sea lanes to China better than they knew the land route to Boston. It is a heritage that has enriched and sustained us for generations, teaching us resilience, a certain measure of stoicism, and a fine regard for the integrity of craft.

Hard at Work and Prospering

Jim Coogan

Published just three years before the opening of the American Civil War, the 1858 map of the Cape and Islands showcases the region's pride and confidence at midcentury. And that is what New York engraver Henry F. Walling and his subscribers intended. Featured along with the familiar geography are lithographs depicting prominent institutional and civic landmarks. Provincetown's preeminence on Cape Cod is marked by a bustling shore scene and a picture of its magnificent harbor, home to over two-dozen busy wharfs. The impressive Barnstable County Courthouse, with its Greek Revival design, anchors the southeast corner of the map. The Pacific Bank of Nantucket and the Barnstable Bank of Yarmouth Port occupy the opposite corner. The former image contributes a sense of the region's social and legal stability. The latter symbolizes the economic vitality that marked both Cape Cod and the Islands in this time period. There is a view of the Customs House in Barnstable, only two years old in 1858, where issues related to maritime commerce were transacted for the county. Even private residences are detailed. The images all point toward an orderly and disciplined populace secure in their communities, hard at work, and prospering.

A look at the business directories spaced around the map shows dry goods and clothing dealers, hardware and grocery stores, millinery shops, restaurants, and dealers in watches and jewelry. There are public houses, furniture dealers, and fancy goods stores. These listings reflect a modern citizenry, comfortable in material things—a people taking a back seat to no one. The Great Age of Sail is still in its heyday, and the situation of the maritime trade is summed up in advertisements for importers of sperm oil, ship's chandlers, and sail makers. And certainly the map's sizeable list of Cape and Islands lawyers can be taken as a measure of the region's mid-century vitality.

No longer solely dependent on the sea as a connector to the world beyond, the tracks of the Cape Cod Railroad link the peninsula securely to the rest of the country. Reaching the Cape at Sandwich from Wareham, the tracks continue east along the bay side through Barnstable, ending at the port of Hyannis. In 1858, the railroad was only four years old, but it was already pushing Hyannis to become the economic hub of the Cape. The rails would reach Orleans just seven years later, and by 1873, Provincetown would be part of a complete and dependable transportation system. Ironically, the completion of the railroad freed the Cape from dependence on locally produced goods and hastened the demise of local factories.

But all this would come later. By midcentury, the Cape and Islands population in the three counties together numbered almost fifty thousand residents. Whaling had built the fortunes of both Martha's Vineyard and Nantucket, and even though much of the trade was moving to New Bedford and Fairhaven, the islands, perhaps because so many whaling masters still hailed from these sea-front outposts, continued to control the wealth and reputation of that industry. For all three counties, the decade of the 1850s was probably the high noon of public life, and prominent individuals were in their ascendancy. Barnstable's great jurist, Lemuel Shaw, was in his third decade as a member of the Massachusetts State Supreme Judicial Court. Sea captains like Ezra Nye of Sandwich, Centerville native Josiah Richardson, Joshua Crowell of Dennis, and Allen Knowles of Yarmouth, along with dozens of other master mariners from the area, were celebrated in ports around the world for their skill. Cyrus

Cahoon ruled the mid-Cape as the "cranberry king," and the varieties of glassware—both utilitarian and specialty glass from Deming Jarves's Sandwich factory—were sought after across the nation and, indeed, the world.

The islands too, were still in their ascendancy. Nantucket sported five active wharfs and a population of over five thousand people. The telegraph cable to the mainland was just two years old. Even though the larger whale ships were having difficulty entering the harbor, Main Street sparkled with new brick homes along gaslit streets, and further evidence of prosperity could be seen in the island's two newspapers, an active Athenaeum, and the presence of three doctors in practice there. The new Academy Hill School, built at a cost of $20,000, had just opened. The Vineyard was no less wanting in prosperous ship owners and whaling captains. But like its island rival the Gray Lady, its future was already moving toward an economy based on attracting summer visitors. The religious campground was witnessing conversions by the hundreds, and each August, some fifty preachers and as many as six thousand people were present on the Sabbath. Promoters of real estate interests were touting the island's excellent climate and were encouraging wealthy mainlanders to build summer homes.

A close look at the map will show a few features that might surprise contemporary observers. The Cape Cod Canal is absent—still an unfulfilled dream. Scheme after scheme to build the waterway had come to naught—and the project would defy success for almost another half century. Vineyard Haven cannot be found on Martha's Vineyard. In 1858, it was called Holmes' Hole. The town of Oak Bluffs has not yet separated from Edgartown and is called Eastville. There is no town of Bourne on the Cape; Sandwich would eventually give a grudging birth to that town in 1884. Mashpee remains a district, set aside for Native Americans but not controlled by them. A section of West Brewster is called Factory Village, a prosperous and well-defined community where the flow of Stony Brook provided enough water power to sustain several small-scale industries. Billingsgate Island off the bayside Wellfleet coast is shown as the active community of resident fishermen that it was when the map was printed. A sharp eye will note that there is a telegraph office in Yarmouth Port and elsewhere. More links to the outside world had arrived.

Certainly the map's engraver could not see the future when he put it together. His intent was to capture what was—not what would be. But even if the future wasn't a concern for him, he was unwittingly prescient. One of the ships pictured on the map is a full-rigged clipper ship, graceful and beautiful, but already obsolete. The other is powered by steam, the type of vessel that would bring the curtain down on the Age of Sail in less than a decade. Interestingly, both ships are pictured heading away from the Atlantic Ocean. The great West was already calling; and in the decades after the Civil War, that outward pull away from the worn-out east coast would tear much of the heart out of what the Cape and Islands were in earlier times. The War of the Rebellion, as it would be called in the North, was only three years away. And with its calamitous effect on the shipping industry, the conflict would begin the slow transformation of the Cape and Islands from a vibrant and expanding region to what the area would become by the end of the century—a largely forgotten backwater of small farms run by women and old men, a place fit only for inspiring nostalgic themes for artists and writers about its past days of greatness.

The 1858 map is a valuable resource for historians in explaining the evolution of the Cape and Islands over a broad span of time. It provides us with a snapshot of the values and ideals that were related to this specific place in time. As such, it gives us an important point to measure the changing life of the region, not only as it was in the mid-nineteenth century, but as it would eventually become in the future.

Exploring the Shores
of Cape Cod and the Islands

Elliott Carr

While viewing Henry Walling's historic 1858 map, my eyes travel immediately to Factory Village, my "home village" in West Brewster, where Stony Brook passes under a heavily trafficked road. Factory Village is listed in the National Register of Historic Places, but most people passing through focus primarily on a bucolic rural herring run. Each spring, volunteers dutifully count herring: antique relics of Cape Cod's first regulated industry.

On Walling's map, Stony Brook is labeled "herring river." Henry Thoreau presciently commented in the 1850s that there are "so many herring rivers on the Cape; they will perhaps be more numerous than herring soon." But Factory Village also served as one of the Cape's major industrial areas. Industry was lured by power from the Cape's steepest water drop: twenty-four feet over numerous small waterfalls. And the village hosted a school, a store, and a tannery, in addition to the still-operating gristmill. Cape Codders of the day couldn't afford to overlook the power of even modest waterfalls.

Departing Factory Village on the map, I make a visual perambulation of the Cape shoreline. I walked the entire shoreline of Cape Cod in 1995 (including swimming or wading across every inlet), so I have some knowledge of it. Comparing what I know it to be now with that depicted on the 1858 map, it is clear that for each village and harbor, change characterizes the past 150 years.

Monomoy Island, south of Chatham, changes every year, sometimes every month, as the area dons a new bathing suit. Walling's map includes twelve small channels through the southern end of Nauset Beach, now South Beach. Those channels are all long-since filled by the never-ending flow of sand from the north. Whitewash Village at Powder Hole Harbor near Monomoy's southern tip was once home to two hundred people and Public School #13, but on Walling's map, it is noted only by the "Lovelands & Thachers Store" and "Read & Lewis Store." Maybe Walling intuited the village would be abandoned several years later after a severe hurricane.

At Monomoy and most other places on Cape Cod's shoreline perimeter, nature—and technology—move inexorably on, frequently forcing man, who seems to have had more common sense back in 1858, to retreat.

Scanning north from Monomoy, Nauset Beach remained unbroken between Chatham and Orleans on the map, with no "cuts" like those opened by ocean storms in 1987 and 2007. However, a narrow channel from Town Cove to Pleasant Bay separated the upper end of the beach from mainland Orleans.

Hatch's Harbor in Provincetown and East Harbor in Truro once served as active fishing ports. In 1868, East Harbor (barricaded from Cape Cod Bay by first a railroad trestle and then a road, and renamed Pilgrim Lake) began over a century of increasing stagnation, as "Beach Point" became just another stretch of shoreline between road and water.

A dike converted Duck Harbor in Wellfleet, where another Herring River flowed into Wellfleet Harbor, into a wetland and part of a golf course.

Recently, the National Seashore has been working to restore the natural flow of water to Hatch's Harbor, East Harbor, and Wellfleet's Herring River.

Two jetties converted a wider natural V-shaped harbor into a channel at Sesuit Harbor in East Dennis. This is where Shiverick Boat Yard built and launched the clipper ship *Christopher Hall* the year this map was published. Builders could only float ships out of the harbor in March, during the highest tide of each year. East Dennis is also where John Sears built the first saltworks in 1777. Sears created eight bushels of salt in his first year carrying the water in buckets, then thirty the next year utilizing a converted bilge pump. But the saltworks that dot Walling's map produced $236,178 of salt for trade according to the State Census of 1855.

A man-made breakwater that protected Brewster's packet landing is indicated on the 1858 map. Today remnants of the breakwater can still be seen, along with a few well-preserved boards. Much of the town's trade flowed on and off through the landings.

In the largest change of all, the U.S. Army Corps of Engineers expanded Monument River into the Cape Cod Canal, using the dredged material to construct a causeway out to Mashnee Island in Buzzards Bay.

A much greater tidal range and the furor of the open ocean changed the Atlantic and Cape Cod Bay shorelines represented in Walling's map more than comparatively benign Nantucket Sound and Buzzards Bay, which are subject only to the furor of occasional hurricanes. The Cape's worst, in 1944, consumed forty feet of Wianno shoreline, after which a state official suggested building a wall around the entire Cape.

My three strongest impressions from Walling's map pertain to the region as a whole.

First, in 1858, there weren't many houses on the Cape Cod shoreline; almost all occupied inland roads. The local population, which worked at or on the water, knew better than to build houses exposed to shorefront "weather." Many modest working buildings on the waterfront were constructed to be rolled back to accomodate changing shoreline.

Second, everything everywhere bore names reflecting the maritime economy. Every navigatable river or cove bore the name harbor or port. Other places included fish names, led by the granddaddy of all—Cod—a cornerstone of the entire Massachusetts economy that became the state's symbol. All told, fisheries provided $1,501,095 of the region's income in 1855, as indicated on the statistical table on the 1858 map. When combined with the associated activity of manufacturing whale products such as candles and oil, which produced income of $1,267,159, they compose a full 60 percent of the region's income.

Like herring, the cod population lags far behind former numbers, subject to ever-increasing regulation.

Finally "villages," each built around their own church, fit the dictionary definition—clusters of houses separated by open space. Now the term carries only romantic meaning, the clusters being largely indistinguishable when driving from one to the next.

On today's Cape and Islands, a growing ring of opulent homes walls in an inland increasingly like everywhere else. The innovative and hyperactive maritime economy of 1858 has given way to a far more passive, landscape-consuming, recreational economy.

Henry Walling's map paints a very rich picture of Cape Cod. But a tinge of sadness blurs the view. No one would have planned or zoned for today's Cape Cod in 1858, or indeed in 1958, shortly after so-called planners sliced and diced the Cape using zoning models created for suburban Boston's needs. The map of 2058 will look considerably better if we step back to consider how to shape growth, rather than continue to analyze one project at a time.

Creating a Community Bank in the 1850s

Theresa Mitchell Barbo

In 1858, Henry F. Walling released his famously detailed *Map of the Counties of Barnstable, Dukes and Nantucket, Massachusetts*. The approximately five-foot-by-five-foot chart revealed more than the geographic contours of Cape Cod, Martha's Vineyard, and Nantucket. The document confirmed that the region had blossomed from the seeds of a series of colonial outposts to defined and prosperous seaside towns and villages.

On Thursday, June 10, 1858, for example, the bow of the fishing schooner *Golden Eagle* dug in and rose with the seas of Cape Cod Bay toward East Dennis to offload mackerel bound for local supper plates. Day fishermen hoisted anchor from Harwich, Martha's Vineyard, and Chatham, all bound for Nantucket Sound and nearby rich banks, where seemingly endless schools of cod, flounder, skate, and herring congregated. Coastal packets on Cape Cod Bay carried nineteenth-century "commuters" who sailed from Barnstable or Yarmouth to Boston. Southside packets lined Nantucket Sound and sailed to New York, Providence, and Newport. Whaling vessels headed for distant waters in the South Pacific. Merchant sea captains from the region sailed around the world delivering every sort of cargo to distant ports.

It was within this maritime-oriented climate that a group of intrepid Cape Codders established the Cape Cod Five Cents Savings Bank (now known as Cape Cod Five) and its "sister institution," the Cape Cod Bank, which eventually became part of a larger bank and no longer exists. The Cape Cod Five Cents Savings Bank, as its name indicates, began as a "savings bank" accepting deposits as small as a nickel. The first bank building is on the Harwich Center inset of the 1858 map with the name "Cape Cod Bank" written next to it. The original building survives as part of the Town of Harwich's Brooks Free Library.

Historian Joan M. Maloney, in her wonderful history, *Community Life*, published in 2001, offers insight on Harwich and the founding of Cape Cod Five Cents Savings Bank. Her research shows that the cofounders were smart, sophisticated people who understood that their vision would outlive their physical lives.

The chartering of the bank was primarily—although certainly not solely—the result of the efforts of the Brooks family of Harwich, from which the Brooks Free Library receives its name. Key family members included Obed Brooks Sr., who operated a general store in Harwich Center that had been established by his father, Ebinezer Brooks. Like many Cape Codders of the time, Obed Brooks Sr. and his wife, Sally (Weeks) Brooks, had a large family of eleven children. Obed Brooks Sr. was active in community life, serving at various times as the captain of a local militia company, town clerk and treasurer, justice of the peace, federal postmaster, and county judge. By the time the bank was chartered in 1855, Obed Brooks Sr. was not well, having suffered a stroke in 1852 that left him seriously incapacitated. He died in 1856.

Of his three sons to survive to adulthood, Obed Brooks Jr. (the eldest) probably played the most important role in establishing the bank. Obed Brooks Jr. had taken over the family store. Like many local business people, he found it challenging to operate without the support of a local bank to provide cash during lean times. This was especially true during the winter, when many fishermen, farmers, and traders found themselves strapped for cash—a situation that is not unlike that of many Cape Codders and Islanders today. It seems Brooks was not entirely pleased with the then-nearest local bank, the Barnstable Bank, located in Yarmouth Port. Not only was it an inconvenient distance from his store, but many also thought the Barnstable Bank used its financial influence to steer public money toward its part of the region and away from places like Harwich. Certainly, the Barnstable Bank was a powerful local institution, as evinced by the fact that it paid to have a sketch of its building included on the 1858 map. Like the Cape Cod Bank, the Barnstable Bank has long since been merged into larger institutions and no longer exists. Of the three institutions, only the Cape Cod Five Cents Savings Bank continues today.

The establishment of the Cape Cod Five Cents Savings Bank was also supported by the youngest of the three Brooks brothers, Henry C. Brooks, described as a "financial wizard." He was the owner of a successful Boston-based business with international dealings. Henry served as a liaison for the banks to various state and other agencies in Boston. The middle brother of the three, Sidney Brooks, was also an incorporator of the bank and served as its first vice president. He is better known as the founder of Brooks Academy, a notable place of learning on the Cape, operated in Harwich Center from 1844 to 1866.

Other important cofounders included Chester Snow, a nephew of Obed Brooks Sr. The first president of the bank was Nathan Underwood. William H. Underwood was secretary, and Obed Brooks Jr. served as both treasurer and as cashier. Captain Nathaniel Snow, a Chatham saltworks owner, would become the bank's second president in January 1858.

Twenty-six men were invited to become trustees. According to Maloney, "They were drawn from the towns of Hyannis (1), Yarmouth (3), Dennis (5), Chatham (2), Orleans (2), and Harwich (13). Their ranks included an attorney, a physician, a minister, a teacher, a fish inspector, and a builder." Two owned saltworks, five were mariners, one was a cobbler, and several were merchants.

The Cape Cod Five Cents Savings Bank received its charter in 1855. When the bank opened the following year, many locals opened accounts, including John Burk, a twenty-nine-year-old Irish laborer, who used his life savings ($260) to open the bank's first account.

The second person to open an account was Delna Ellis, a housewife, who deposited $2. "Anna Eldredge, a domestic, deposited $1.50 for safe keeping," says Maloney. Isaac Smith, a prosperous butcher, put $600 in the name of his daughter. Indeed, many parents opened accounts for their children to help them learn the values of savings and thrift. Abel Ellis, a farmer, gave his young sons 6¢ and 12¢ respectively to open their own accounts. In all, some 142 accounts had been opened by the end of the first calendar year. Maloney writes, "it is a sign of the times that Brooks knew each of them so well that he recorded only names without identifying addresses."

The bank, like the rest of the region, has grown tremendously in the more than a century and a half that has passed since, but both retain something significant from the times depicted on the 1858 map. It was a period when local town and village communities were vital, yet—thanks to the region's maritime prowess—many also thought globally. From its inception in 1855, the Cape Cod Five Cents Savings Bank nurtured a belief in this unique region and the people who call it home. The founders knew that even a nickel was a worthy deposit, a humble denomination by which to launch a dream and plan for the future.

The Complete Map
and General Items

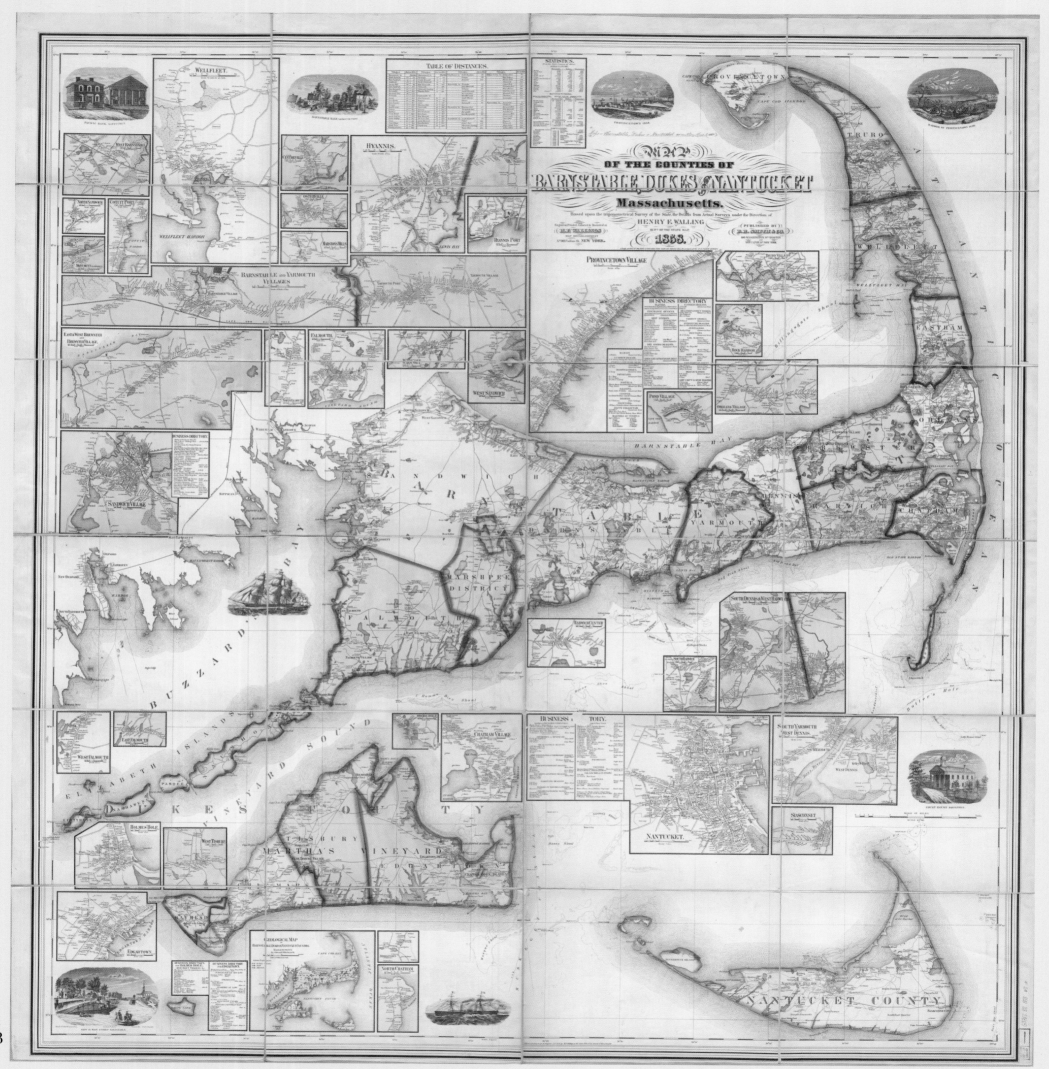

TABLE OF DISTANCES.

Villages.	Dist in Miles.		Villages.	Dist in Miles.	
Monument to		Total Dist.	**Monument to**		Total Dist.
North Sandwich	3.2	3.2	Pocassett	2.3	3.3
West Sandwich	1.5	4.7	South Pocassett	2.0	5.3
Sandwich	2.3	7.0	North Falmouth	2.0	7.3
Spring Hill	2.0	9.0	West Falmouth	3.0	10.3
East Sandwich	1.5	10.5	Falmouth	3.5	13.8
West Barnstable	3.5	14.5	Falmouth Landing	1.2	15.0
Barnstable	5.0	19.0	Woods Hole	3.5	18.0
Yarmouth Port	2.8	21.3			
Yarmouth	1.2	22.5	**Falmouth to**		
Dennis	3.5	26.0	East Falmouth	3.5	3.5
East Dennis	2.0	28.0	Waquoit	3.0	6.5
West Brewster	2.5	30.5	Cotuit	5.3	11.8
Brewster	1.5	32.0	Marstons Mills	2.2	14.0
East Brewster	1.5	33.5	Centreville	4.0	18.0
Orleans	4.0	37.5	Hyannis	3.5	21.5
Eastham	4.3	41.8	West Yarmouth	3.0	24.5
Fresh Brook	4.2	46.0	West Dennis	3.2	27.7
South Wellfleet	1.2	47.2	West Harwich	3.0	30.7
North Wellfleet	1.8	49.0	Harwich Port	2.3	33.0
Truro	4.5	53.5	South Harwich	1.7	34.7
Pond Village	2.5	56.0	West Chatham	2.7	37.4
North Truro	0.7	56.7	Chatham	2.6	40.0
Provincetown	6.3	63.0			

Villages.	Dist in Miles
Chatham to North Chatham	27
" Orleans	92
" Brewster	105
Harwich to Brewster	55
" East Harwich	35
" Orleans	90
" South Harwich	15
" Harwich Port	13
" West Harwich	28
" South Dennis	42
" Dennis	85
" Yarmouth	80
Hyannis to Hyannis Port	17
" Yarmouth Port	40
" Barnstable	35
" West Barnstable	67
Sandwich to South Sandwich	65
" Cotuit	100
" Cotuit Port	115
" Falmouth Landing	115
" Woods Hole	210

Villages.	Dist in Miles
Edgartown to Holmes Hole	8.0
" West Tisbury	8.5
" Woods Hole	14.0
" Falmouth	14.0
" Cotuit Port	17.0
" Hyannis Port	19.5
" West Dennis	26.0
" West Harwich	29.0
" Harwich Port	32.0
" Chatham	33.5
" Nantucket	25.5
Nantucket to Siasconset	7.5
" Chatham	28.5
" Harwich Port	26.5
" West Harwich	26.6
" West Dennis	27.0
" Hyannis Port	26.0
" Centerville	28.5
" Cotuit Port	29.0
" Waquoit	32.5
" Falmouth	34.0
" Edgartown	27.0
" Holmes Hole	33.0

Horses
Cows & Oxen
Sheep
Swine
Butter lbs.
Cheese
Indian Corn
Wheat
Rye
Barley
Oats
Potatoes
Turnips
Onions
Carrots
Hay

ARTICLES

Woollen Goods
Wrought Iron
Cast
Machinery
Tacks & Brads
Glass
Boats
Shipping
Salt
Carriages
Sperm Candles
Tin Ware
Leather
Boots & Shoes

Sperm & Whale
Mackerel & Cod
Alewives, Shad
Total Value

Barnstable
Brewster
Chatham
Dennis
Eastham
Falmouth
Harwich
Orleans
Provincetown
Sandwich
Truro

70°35′   70°30′

19

WELLFLEET.

PACIFIC BANK, NANTUCKET.

BARNSTABLE BANK, YARMOUTH PORT.

TABLE OF DISTANCES.

WEST BARNSTABLE

HYANNIS.

CENTREVILLE

NORTH SANDWICH   COTUIT PORT

OSTERVILLE

MONUMENT (SANDWICH)

WELLFLEET HARBOR

MARSTON'S MILLS

HYANNIS P...

LEWIS BAY

BARNSTABLE AND YARMOUTH VILLAGES

BARNSTABLE VILLAGE

YARMOUTH VILLAGE

YARMOUTH PORT

CAPE COD RAIL ROAD

EAST & WEST BREWSTER AND BREWSTER VILLAGE.

FALMOUTH.

WEST SANDWICH

BARNSTABLE   BAY

NORTH FALMOUTH

VINEYARD   SOUND

TREMONT

NORTH SANDWICH

WEST SANDWICH

SANDWICH VILLAGE

BUSINESS DIRECTORY.

SANDWICH VILLAGE

MILL POND

WAREHAM   AGAWAM

OLD LANDING

SIPPICAN

SIPPICAN HARBOR

MATTAPOISETT

OXFORD

20

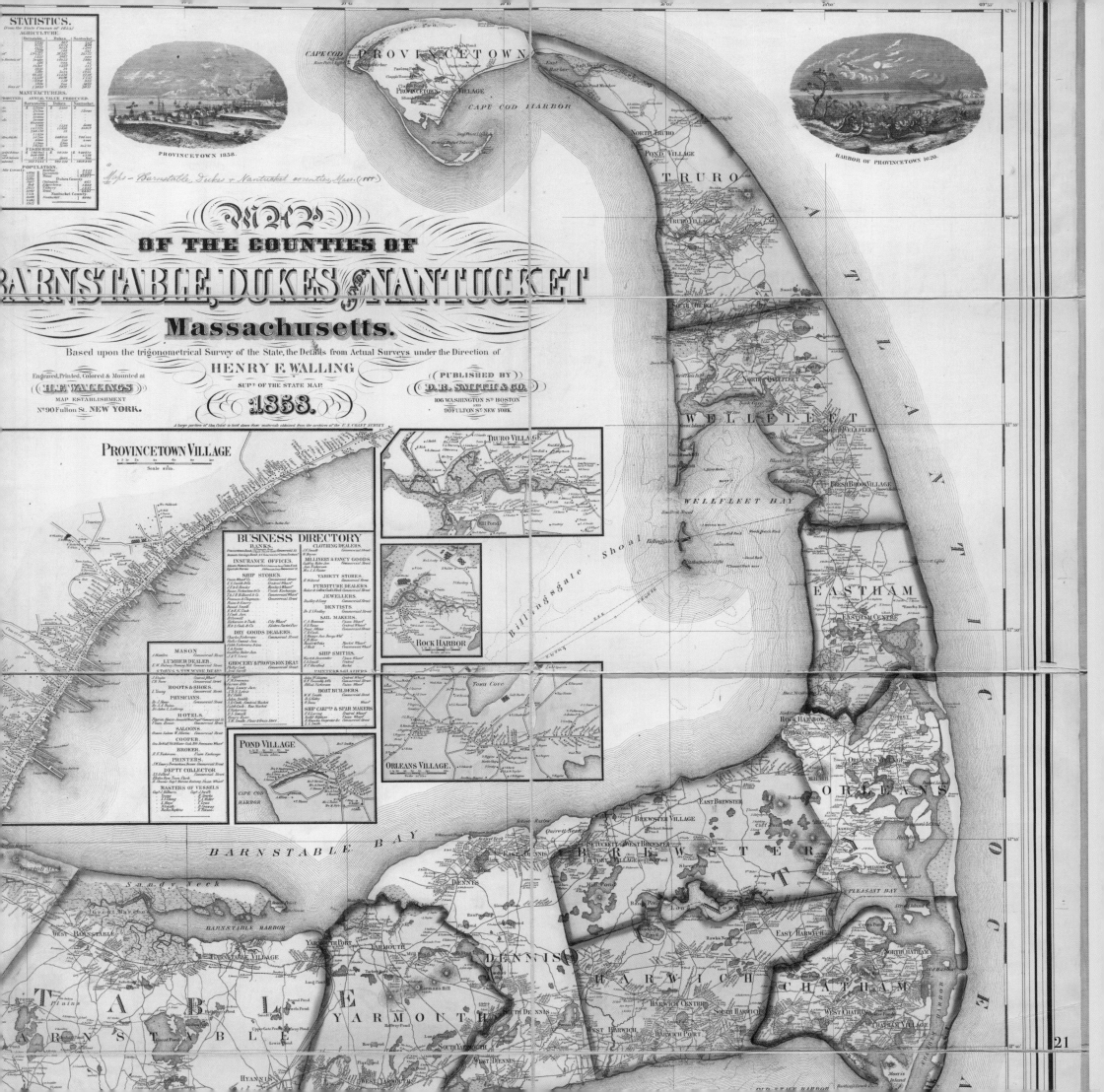

MAP OF THE COUNTIES OF BARNSTABLE, DUKES AND NANTUCKET

Massachusetts.

Based upon the trigonometrical Survey of the State, the Details from Actual Surveys under the Direction of

HENRY F. WALLING

SUP.T OF THE STATE MAP.

Engraved, Printed, Colored & Mounted at

H.F. WALLING'S

MAP ESTABLISHMENT

No. 90 Fulton St. NEW YORK.

PUBLISHED BY

D.R. SMITH & CO.

106 WASHINGTON ST. BOSTON

AND

90 FULTON ST. NEW YORK.

1858.

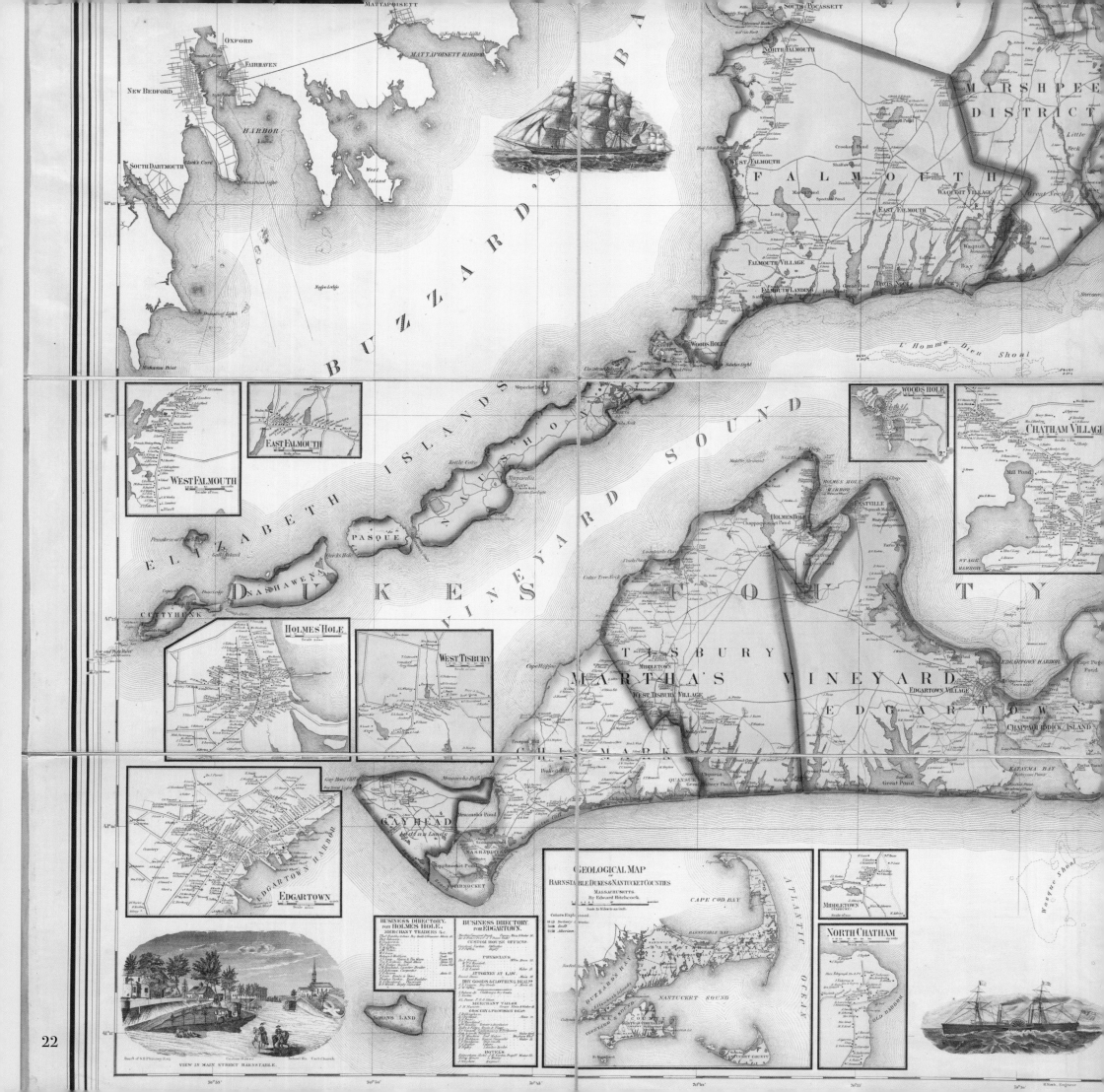

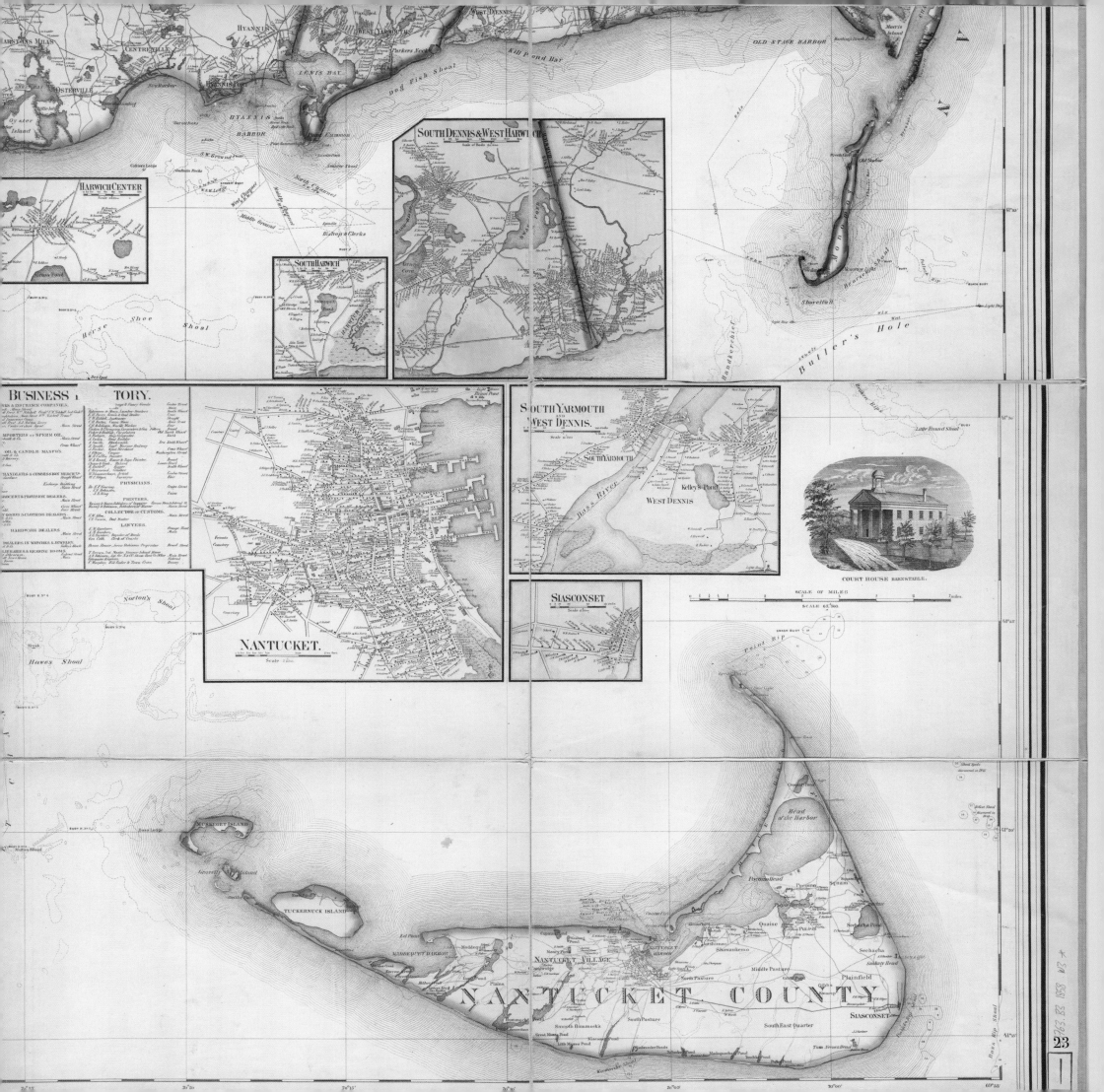

	Dist in Miles
...es Hole	8.0
...Tisbury	8.5
...'s Hole	14.0
...outh	14.0
...t Port	17.0
...nis Port	19.5
...Dennis	26.0
...Harwich	29.0
...ich Port	32.0
...ham	35.5
...cket	25.5
...onset	7.5
...am	28.5
...ich Port	26.5
...Harwich	26.8
...Dennis	27.0
...nis Port	26.0
...erville	28.5
...d Port	29.0
...oit	32.5
...outh	34.0
...artown	27.0
...es Hole	33.0

STATISTICS.

(From the State Census of 1855.)

AGRICULTURE.

	Barnstable.	Dukes.	Nantucket.
Horses	2235	367	346
Cows & Oxen	6221	1692	874
Sheep	1477	9132	1201
Swine	1378	146	541
Butter lbs. of	194327	28382	24152
Cheese	1325	3987	000
Indian Corn Bushels of	70480	16023	7980
Wheat	526	000	25
Rye	1430l	1379	117
Barley	1935	34	552
Oats	7380	3024	1254
Potatoes	66337	11526	7776
Turnips	12159	6498	7752
Onions	5238	158	935
Carrots	7920	700	5635
Hay Tons of	13833	2821	2851

MANUFACTURERS.

ARTICLES PRODUCED.	ANNUAL VALUE PRODUCED.		
	Barnstable.	Dukes.	Nantucket.
Woollen Goods	$ 23000	$ 3400	$.
Wrought Iron	„ 24700		12000
Cast	„ 30000		
Machinery	„ 10000		
Tacks & Brads	„ 20000		
Glass	„ 600000		
Boats	„ 1168	1536	5068
Shipping	„ 147724	11850	20911
Salt	„ 236178	37	
Carriages	„ 11820		
Sperm Candles, Oil &c.	„ 10200	468855	788104
Tin Ware	„ 9900	200	4000
Leather	„ 11900	2500	
Boots & Shoes	„ 19240	3068	10276

FISHERIES.

	Barnstable.	Dukes.	Nantucket.
Sperm & Whale Oil & Bone	$ 196903	$ 49350	$ 429870
Mackerel & Cod	„ 806386		4228
Alewives, Shad & Salmon	„ 11258	3000	700
Total Value Produced	„ 3092442	762232	1608800

POPULATION.

Barnstable County.

Barnstable	4996	Wellfleet	2325
Brewster	1525	Yarmouth	2592
Chatham	2560	Total	35877
Dennis	3497	**Dukes County.**	
Eastham	808	Chilmark	667
Falmouth	2613	Edgartown	1898
Harwich	3261	Tisbury	1827
Orleans	1754	Total	4401
Provincetown	3096	**Nantucket County.**	
Sandwich	4495	Nantucket	8890
Truro	1917		

PROV...

Maps — Barnsta...

Mrs. Baxter

E. Baker

D. ...

...Hallet

24

Store

Grist Mill

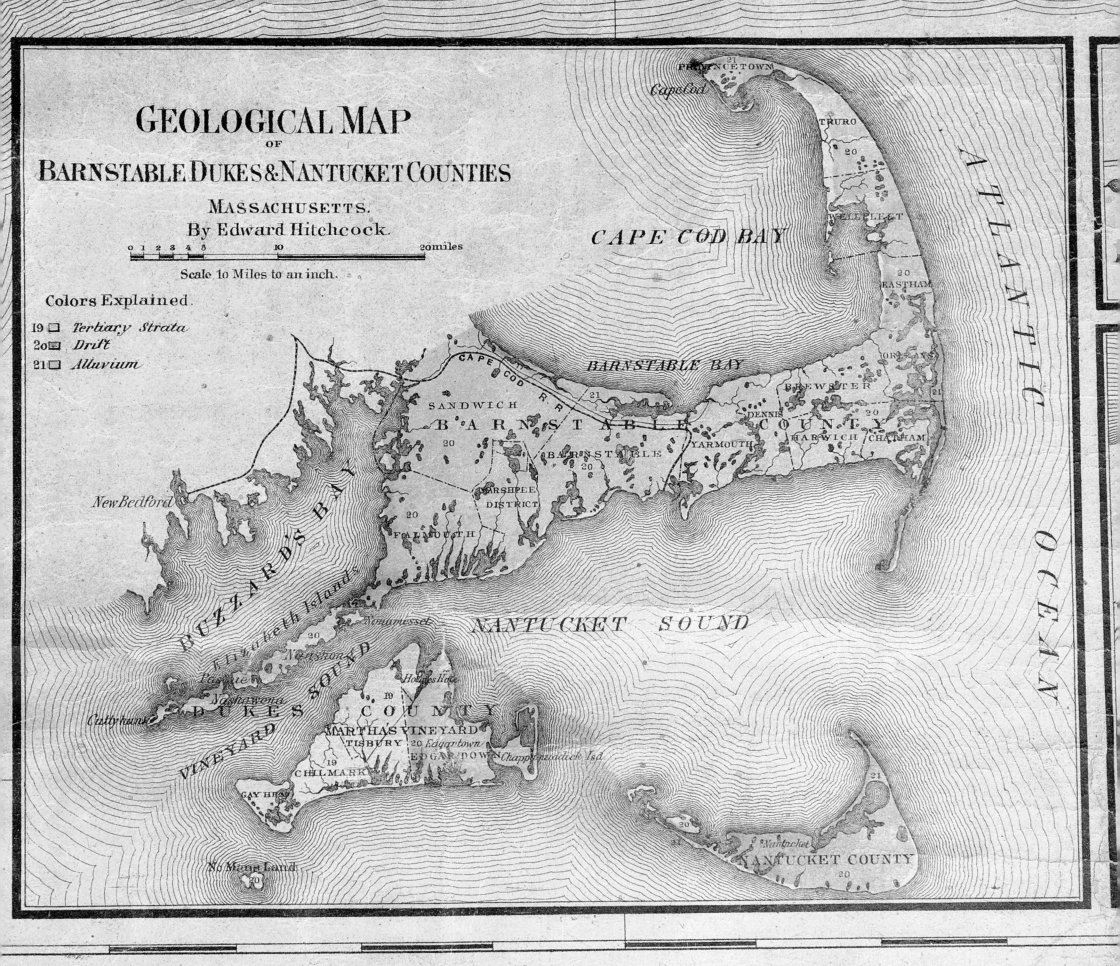

GEOLOGICAL MAP

OF

BARNSTABLE DUKES & NANTUCKET COUNTIES

MASSACHUSETTS.
By Edward Hitchcock.

0 1 2 3 4 5   10   20miles

Scale 1o Miles to an inch.

Colors Explained.

19 ☐ *Tertiary Strata*
2o ☐ *Drift*
21 ☐ *Alluvium*

New Bedford

CAPE COD BAY

BARNSTABLE BAY

BUZZARD'S BAY

SANDWICH

BARNSTABLE COUNTY

DENNIS

BREWSTER

HARWICH   CHATHAM

YARMOUTH

MARSHPEE DISTRICT

FALMOUTH

Elizabeth Islands

Nonamesset

NANTUCKET SOUND

Naushon

Pasque

Holmes Hole

Nashawena

Cuttyhunk

DUKES COUNTY

VINEYARD SOUND

19

MARTHA'S VINEYARD

TISBURY   20 *Edgartown*

EDGARTOWN

Chappaquiddick Isd.

CHILMARK

GAY HEAD

No Mans Land

Nantucket

NANTUCKET COUNTY

A T L A N T I C

O C E A N

PROVINCETOWN

Cape Cod

TRURO

WELLFLEET

EASTHAM

ORLEANS

70°40'

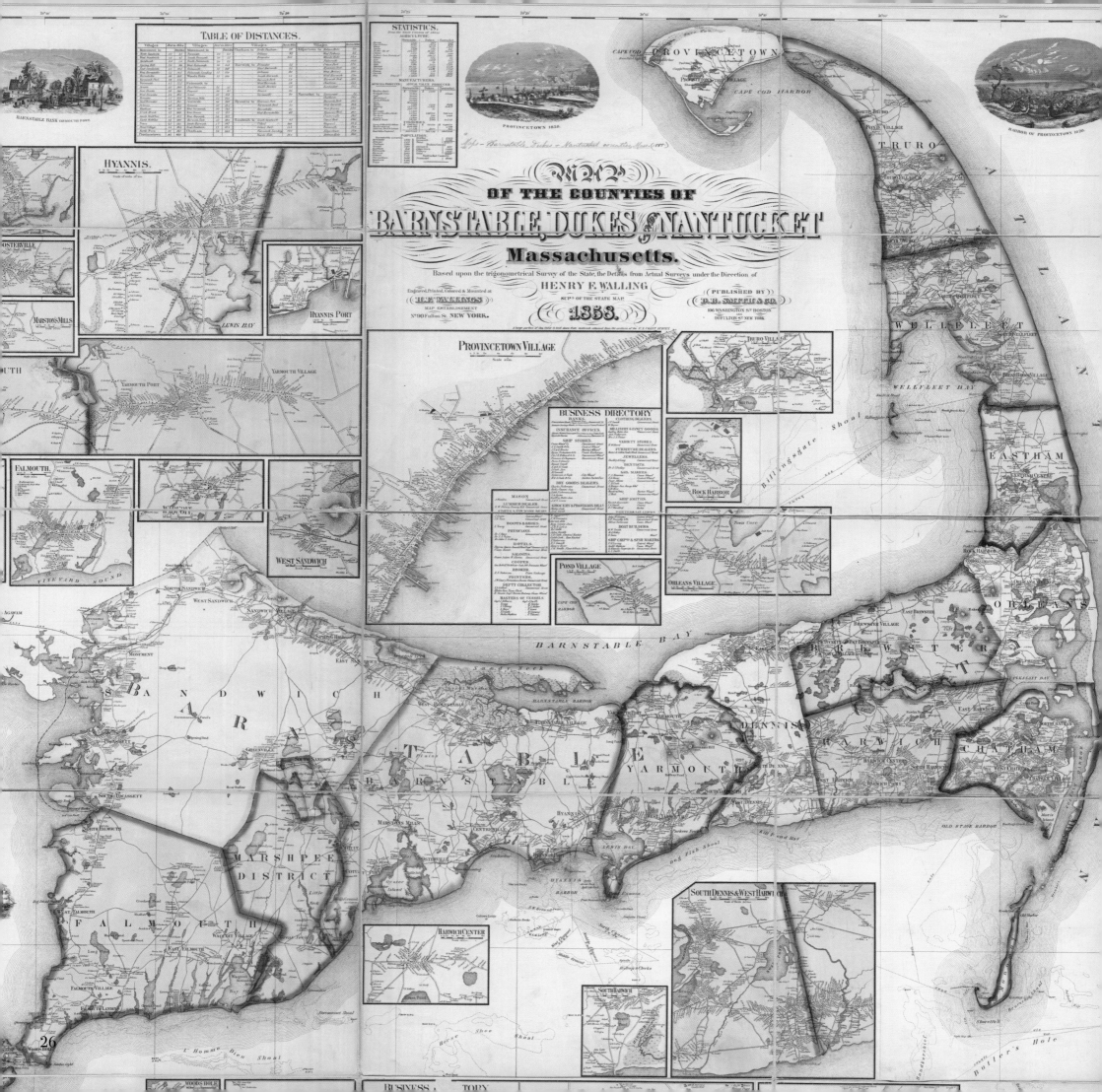

Barnstable County

COURT HOUSE BARNSTABLE.

BUSINESS DIRECTORY.

Boston & Sandwich Glass Co.
Geo. P. Drew, Clothing Store . . . Jarves Street
J. B. Hersey,   "   "   "   "
T. C. Sherman, Dry Goods & Groceries   "
E. R. Cook,   "   "   "   "
Chas. B. Hall, Drug Store & Post Office Main Street
W. H. F. Burbank, Stoves & Tin Ware Jarves   "
Josiah Foster, Cooper, Brass &c.   Main
Wm. E. Boyden, Cape Cod Express.
J. W. Pope, Furniture Dealer   Boydens Block
J. W. Crocker, Restaurant .   "   "
Obed M. Fish, Saloon . . . . Jarves Street
M. Monahan, Dry Goods & Groceries   "
W. F. Bicknell & Co. Provision Store   "
T. F. Atkins Millinery Store . .   "   "
Joseph French, Cooper . . . Summer Str.
Wm. Atkins,   "   "   Main Street
T. Hamblin, Truckman . . . .
W. N. Bassett, Carpenter . . . Liberty   "
G. W. L. Hatch, Planing Mill .
Dr. Julius Thompson, Physician & Den.st Lorings Block
Dr. John Harper, Office & Drug Store   Main Street
E. F. Holway, Lawyer . . . .
Silas Fish, Sandwich Nursery   School   "
S. R. Rogers, Tack Manfry. . . Grove Street
Pinkham & Bawman, Printers   Main   "
B. R. Childs, Sandwich House . . Jarves
Capt. Roland Gibbs, Master of Steamer Acorn
W. C. & I. K. Chipman, Sash & Blind Mfr. Town Hall
F. S. Pope, Store . . . . . Main Street
A. Holway,   "   "   Boydens Block
Wm. E. Boyden, Livery Stable . . Main Street
N. H. Fish, Bakery . . . . . River   "

WEST SANDWICH

Scale 30.000

NORTH SANDWICH

Great Herring Pond

Sagamore Hill

WEST SANDWICH

Manomet
Iron Works

Town Neck

SANDWICH VILLAGE

Spring Hill Creek

SPRING HILL

Apple Grove School

Scorton Harbor

Scorton Neck

EAST SANDWICH

S a n d

Deep Bottom Pond

Great Marshes

N   D   W   I   C   H

WEST BARNSTABLE

A   R

Succonnessett Pond's

Spectacle Pond

Opening Pond

Lawrence
Pond

N

Triangle Pond

S   T   A

Peters Pond

GREENVILLE

Lower Hog Pond
Upper Hog Pond

PONDS
Plains

Snake Pond

SOUTH SANDWICH

NEWTOWN
Mudd Pond

Shubael Pond

Weeks Pond

Pimlico Pond

Purchased Land

Wakeby Pond

Lilly Pond

Long Fond

B   A   R   N   S   T

Bear Hollow

Purchased Land

Long Pond

Marshpee Pond

Santuit Pond

MARSTONS MILLS

Lovells Pond

CENTREV

John's Pond

COTUIT

29

SANDWICH VILLAGE

Mill Pond

Mill River

CAPE COD RAIL ROAD

FRANKLIN ST.

RIVER ST.

MAIN ST.

JARVES ST.

STATE ST.

WILLOW ST.

CROSS ST.

HARBOR ST.

FREEMAN ST.

CANARY ST.

PLEASANT ST.

SUMMER STREET

LIBERTY ST.

SCHOOL ST.

WATER ST.

GROVE ST.

R. R. TO WHARF

Boston & Sandwich Glass Comp.

Glass Co.

Town Hall

Grist Mill

Cemetery

Academy

Tack Factory

Town Farm House

Scale 10.000
0 5 10 20 40 80 rods
¼ mile

N. Dillingham
D. Chase
J. Eldridge
I. Berry
J. Quinby

L. Rogers
E. Parks
L. B. Nye
J. B. Dillingham
B. Sears
E. Nichols
W. Spring
S. Sears
School
Mrs. Wells
W. F. Jones
J. B. Hall
J. H. Faunce
W. H. F. Burbank
F. U. Lovell
O. B. Nye
J. E. Chipman
J. Bassett
T. A. Tobey
W. Fessenden
S. C. Burbank
C. Nye
Mrs. Swift
S. F. Nyes Est.
S. Burbank
Office
Town Hall
Shoe Sh.
Carriage Shop
Market Shop
M. Bourne
Cong. Church
J. & J. Newcomb
N. Crocker &
Dr. Russell
S. R. Rogers
S. Pope
E. T. Pope
W. Loring
A. Fish
T. Nye
J. Whitley
J. Tobey
T. A. Tobey
W. F. Tobey
E. R. Wing
J. Boyden
Miss Smith
W. Fessenden
G. Howland
W. T. Fisher
M. Howland

Mrs. Heffernen
W. & H. T. Bassell
B. S. Shop
N. H. Fish's Bakery
Unitarian Church
Masonic Hall
Furniture Warehouse
Livery Stable
Central Hotel
Restaurant
Cape Cod Express
W. Boyden
N. Howard
H. V. Spurr
T. Kern
A. Kelley
J. Foster
S. Fish
M. Bourne
W. Pope
L. Dillingham
D. C. Percival
Mrs. Boyden
R. T. & J. W. Pope
School
W. Perry
T. Kern
C. F. Eldridge

N. Dillingham
W. Price &
Mrs. Chamberlain
T. Dean
I. Drake
D. Covell
G. F. Lapham
Dr. Leonard
J. Hatch
University Church
R. Tobey
Mrs. Bodfish
C. P. Watermen
I. K. Chipman
C. B. H. Fessenden
N. F. Fessenden

J. Blackwell
F. B. Dillingham
Dr. Bassell
G. Nyes Est.
I. Bates's Est.
L. Gifford
M. Murphy

B. Woods
Clothing Store
Public Hall
Sandwich Bank
Episcopal Church
J. Miller
Mrs. Fish
I. Hatch
H. Allen
Mrs. Southack
Meth. Ch.
W. H. Bassell
E. Baker
F. Woods
F. Wright
W. Smith
M. Tinkham
G. W. L. Hatch
G. W. L. Hatch
M. Tinkham
T. Hamblin
J. A. Holway
R. Gibbs
R. R. Co.

Glass Co. Depot
N. Howard
J. Thompson
Bakers Shop
T. P. Riorden
E. Covell
J. Fisk
W. F. Lapham
J. H. Lapham
F. Nye
C. Allen
W. Kern
J. Black
J. Quinnell
Mrs. Fisk
G. Marston
S. Alton
P. Shevelin
D. Burgess
B. R. Childs
J. French
C. Quinn
T. T. Blackwell
W. N. Bassell
C. F. Hamblin
G. W. L. Hatch

Montague
E. Brady
J. Marsh
Montague
Mrs. Warren
E. Carey
W. Crangle
S. O'Niel
J. McManus
W. Davis
O. Duffee
T. P. Donovan
C. Donovan
Hinckley & Black
School
D. Jarves
Horan
Bradley
J. Harrison
J. Wellard
E. Cadworth
J. W. Jarves
J. Vallier
F. Howland
G. F. Hoxie
R. T. Pope
J. Fuller
B. R. Childs
J. Fish
T. H. Fuller
C. Manson
J. Hartford
C. W. Lapham
G. L. Fessenden
A. Hamblin
A. Stimpson

W. Collins
S. Kern
Mrs. Hobson
J. Barry
J. Rogers
W. Hernden
W. Hobson
J. Barker
E. Kern
T. McLand
J. McKenna
Cath. Church
D. Jarves
C. Bassell
I. Storry
J. Wight
C. Daniels
W. B. H. Kenny
Store
Store
Store
Store

34

MATT

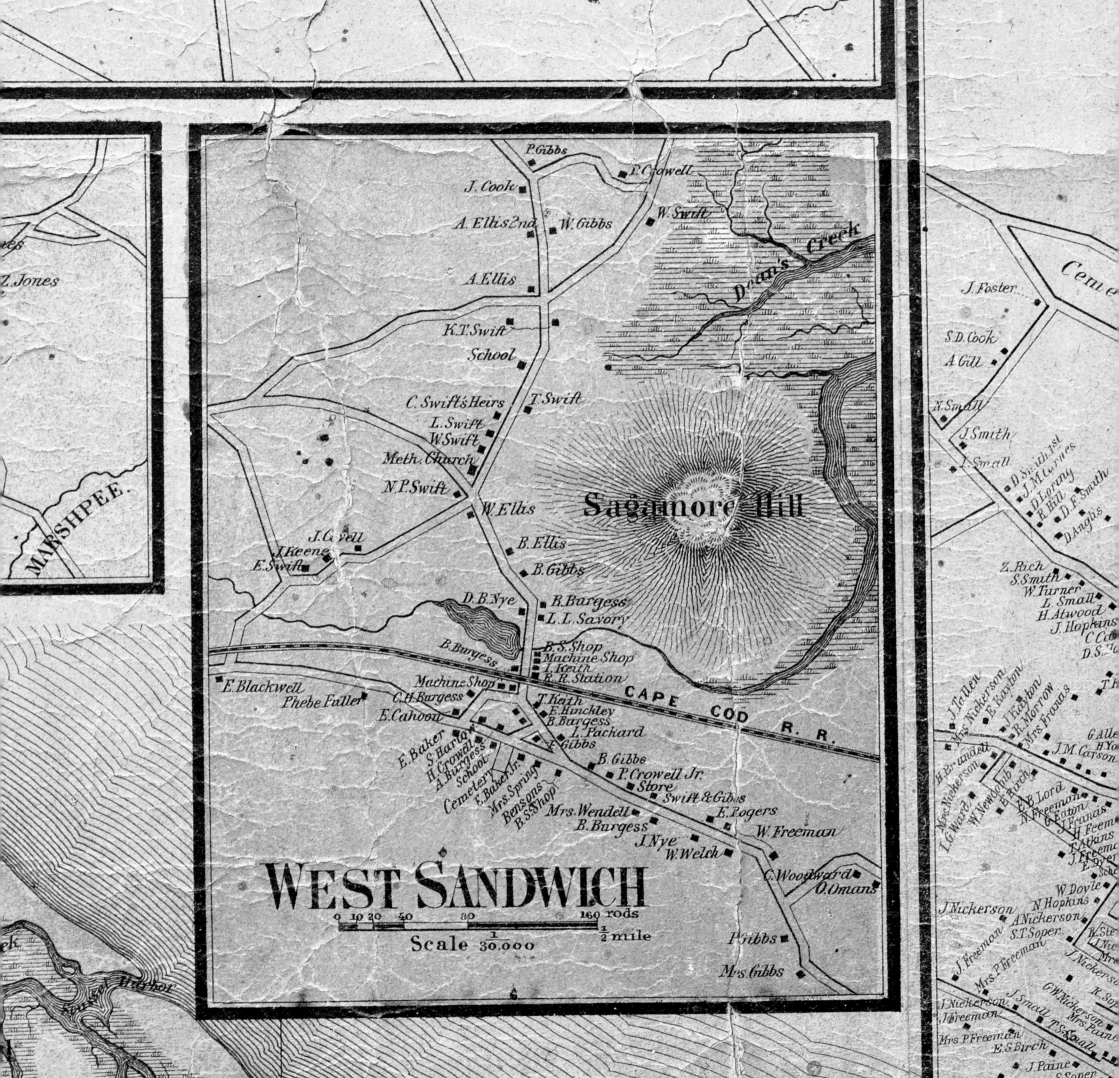

MARSHPEE.

Z. Jones

P. Gibbs
J. Cook
P. Crowell
A. Ellis 2nd   W. Gibbs   W. Swift
A. Ellis
Dean's Creek

K.T. Swift
School

C. Swift's Heirs   T. Swift
L. Swift
W. Swift
Meth. Church
N.P. Swift
W. Ellis

Saganore Hill

B. Ellis
B. Gibbs

J. Covell
J. Keene
E. Swift

D.B. Nye   B. Burgess
L.L. Savory

B. Burgess
B.S. Shop
Machine Shop
I. Keith
E.R. Station

E. Blackwell   Machine Shop
Phebe Fuller   C.H. Burgess   T. Keith
E. Cahoon   E. Hinckley
B. Burgess
E. Baker   L. Packard
S. Harlow   I. Gibbs
H. Crowell   B. Gibbs
A. Burgess   P. Crowell Jr.
School   Store
Cemetery   E. Baker Jr.
E. Baker   Swift & Gibbs
Mrs. Spring
Bensons   E. Rogers
B.S. Shop   Mrs. Wendell
B. Burgess   W. Freeman
J. Nye
W. Welch
C. Woodward
O. Omans
CAPE COD R.R.

WEST SANDWICH

0 10 20   40   80   160 rods
1
Scale ‾‾‾‾‾
30.000   ½ mile

P. Gibbs

Mrs. Gibbs

Cem.
J. Foster
S.D. Cook
A. Gill
N. Small
J. Smith
J. Small   D. Smith 1st
J.M. Carnes
D. Loring
R. Hill
D.F. Smith
D. Anglis
Z. Rich
S. Smith
W. Turner
L. Small
H. Atwood
J. Hopkins
C. Co
D.S.

J. Allen   E. Kaston
Mrs. Nickerson   R. Morrow
Mrs. Froias
H. Brundett   G. Alle
I.G. Ward   J.M. Carson
Mrs. Nickerson   H. Yo
W. Newcomb
J. Birch
E.B. Lord
N. Freeman
G. Eaton
J. Franis
H Freeman
T. Atkins
J. Freema
E. Dye

W. Doyle
J. Freeman   N. Hopkins
J. Nickerson   A. Nickerson
S.T. Soper
Mrs. P. Freeman   R. St
I. Nu
J. Nickers

J. Nickerson   G.W. Nickerson
J. Freeman   J. Small   Mrs. Rat
Mrs. P. Freeman   T.S. Small
E.S. Birch
J. Paine
S. Soper

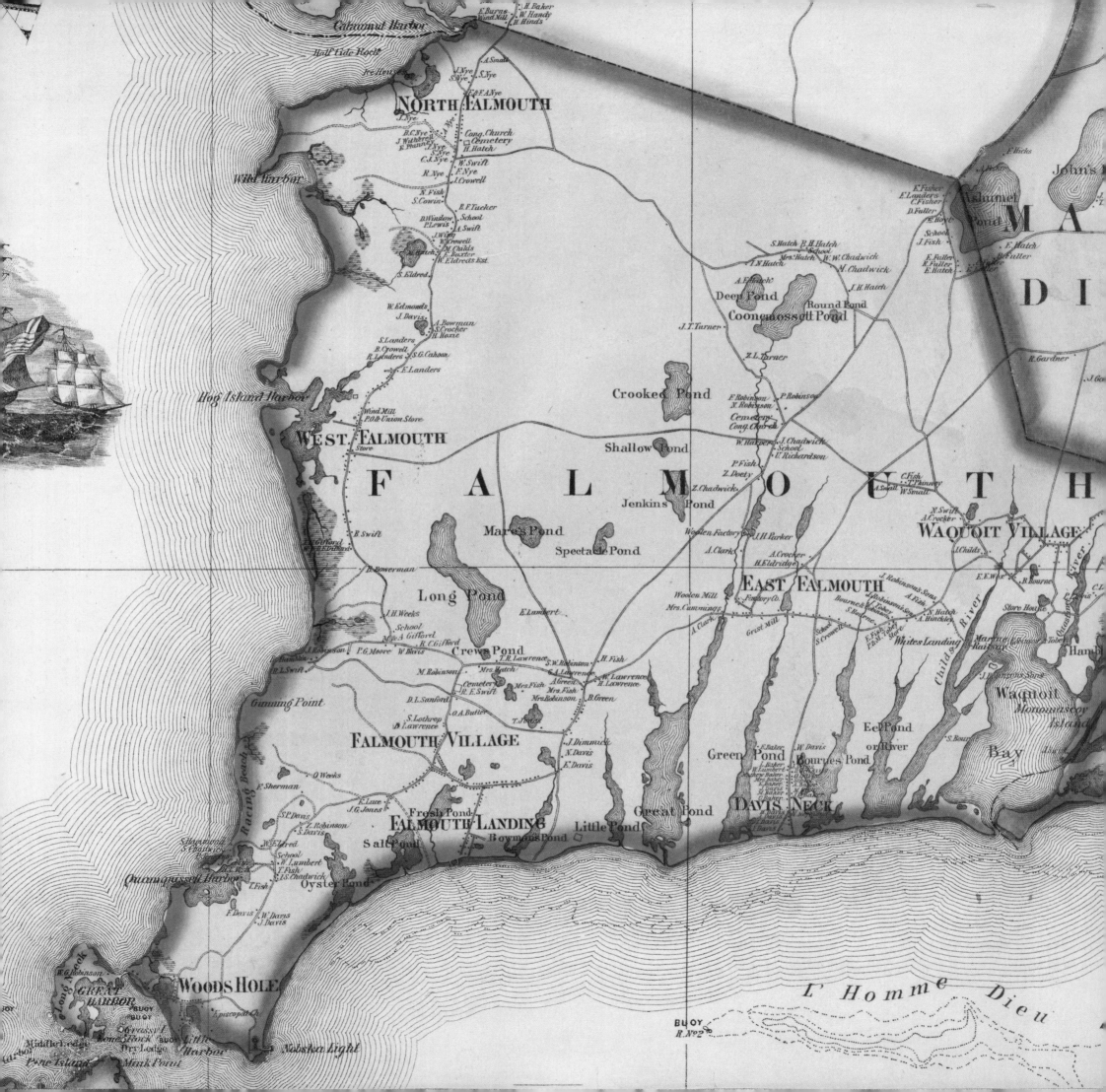

Catamnet Harbor

E. Burne W. Handy
Wind Mill H. Hinds

Half Tide Rock

Ice House

A. Small

J. Nye
S. Nye   S. Nye

F. & F. A. Nye

NORTH FALMOUTH

J. Nye

B. C. Nye   Cong. Church Cemetery
J. Withrell   T. Nye H. Hatch
E. Phinney   T. Nye
C. J. Nye   W. Swift
R. Nye   F. Nye
               J. Crowell

N. Fish
S. Cowin   B. F. Tucker
               School
D. Winslow   A. Swift
E. Lewis
J. Wicu
           N. Crowell
           M. Childs
           E. Baxter
N. Hatch   W. Eldreas Est.

S. Eldred

W. Edmonds
J. Davis   A. Bowman
            S. Crocker
            H. Hoxie
S. Landers
B. Crowell S. G. Cahoon
R. Landers
        E. Landers

Hog Island Harbor

Wind Mill
P. O. & Union Store

WEST FALMOUTH
Store

FALMOUTH

J. Gifford
W. B. E. Dillard

B. Bowerman

B. Swift

Mares Pond
Long Pond

J. H. Weeks
School
Mrs. A. Gifford
R. C. Gifford
J. Robinson P. G. Moore W. Davis Crews Pond
R. L. Swift   T. R. Lawrence
        M. Robinson   Mrs. Hatch
                Cemetery   Mrs. Fish
                R. E. Swift
Gunning Point   D. L. Sanford
            S. Lothrop   O. A. Butler
            J. Lawrence

FALMOUTH VILLAGE

F. Sherman   O. Weeks

S. P. Davis
Z. Robinson
S. Davis
E. Luce
J. G. Jones   Fresh Pond
W. Eldred   ## FALMOUTH LANDING
S. Hammond   Salt Pond
S. Chadwick
School
F. Fish   W. Lumbert
T. Fish   J. S. Chadwick   Oyster Pond
Quamquissett Harbor

F. Davis W. Davis
          J. Davis

W. G. Robinson
Long Neck
GREAT
HARBOR
BUOY

Episcopal Ch.
Middle Ledge   Nome Rock
Dry Ledge   buoy   Little
Pine Island   Mink Point   Harbor   Nobska Light

Spectacle Pond

Jenkins Pond

S. W. Robinson H. Fish
C. A. Lawrence
A. Green   W. Lawrence
           H. Lawrence
Mrs. Robinson   B. Green

T. Jones

J. Dimmick
N. Davis
E. Davis

Little Pond
Bowmans Pond

Great Pond

E. Lumbert

Woolen Mill
Factory Co.
Mrs. Cummings

A. Clark
Grist Mill

Shallow Pond

Woolen Factory J. H. Parker
A. Clark   A. Crocker
                H. Eldridge

EAST FALMOUTH

Green Pond
E. Baker   W. Davis
S. Bither
W. Lumbert
Mrs. Baker
S. Baker
W. Baker
M. Baker
S. Baker

DAVIS NECK

Eel Pond
or River

Bournes Pond

S. Hatch B. H. Hatch
          School
T. N. Hatch Mrs. Hatch W. W. Chadwick
A. F. Hatch   M. Chadwick
                      J. H. Hatch

Deep Pond
Coonemossett Pond   Round Pond

J. T. Turner

Z. L. Turner

Crooked Pond
F. Robinson   P. Robinson
N. Robinson
Cemetery
Cong. Church
W. Harper   J. Chadwick
            School
P. Fish   C. Richardson
Z. Doety
Z. Chadwick
                C. Fish
                T. Phinney
            A. Small W. Small

                N. Swift
                A. Crocker
WAQUOIT VILLAGE
J. Childs

J. Robinson Sons
Bourne & S. Baker J. Robinson Sons
         A. Fish
Bourne S. Tobey N. Hatch
        Johnson A. Hinckley
S. Crowell   School
        E. Fish   Whites Landing
        P. & M. Tobey
                Store
E. E. Weeks   B. Bourne

Store House

Marine
Railway

J. Robinsons Sons

Waquoit
Monomoscoy
Island
Bay

S. Bourne

Ashumet
Pond

MA
DI

John's

F. Wicks

E. Fisher
E. Landers C. Fisher
D. Fuller   E. Hoyt
        School
        J. Fish
            E. Fuller
            R. Fuller E. Hatch
                       E. Fuller B. Fuller
                       E. Hatch

R. Gardner

J. G

L' Homme Dieu

BUOY
R. No 2

BUOY
R. No 2

Childs River

Hamb

FALMOUTH.

0 10 20 40 80 160 rods

Scale 1/30,000   1/2 mile

References.
1. H. F. Shiverick, Paint Shop
2. S. M. Hatch,
3. A. Nye,
4. Mrs. Dimmick,
5. T. Lewis,
6. John Jenkins,
7. Store

Crew's Pond

T. R. Lawrence

S. W. Robinson

H. Fish

Mrs. Hatch

M. Robinson

G. A. Lawrence

A. Green

Mrs. Fish

Cemetery

H. Lawrence
W. Lawrence

R. E. Swift

Mrs Fish

D. L. Sanford

Mrs. Robinson
N. P. Baker
B. Jenkins
D. B. Nye
Harness Shop
J. Lawrence
R. T. Jones

B. Green

E. & H. Robinson

T. Lawrence

E. Lawrence

A. Fish

H. F. Gifford

School

C. Lawrence

S. H. Lothrop

T. Jones
S. Lawrence

I. Fish
A. Lawrence
N. Fish

D. Lawrence
H. Tobey
Mrs. T. Hatch
Rev. H. B. Hooker
J. H. Starbuck
S. Jones
H. C. Bunker
J. Butler
E. Butler

H. Robinson
S. P. Crowell
R. S. Wood
D. Hatch
W. N. Bourne
Dr. Rogers Office
O. C. Swift
Pond Church
E. Gould

J. Dimmick

N. Davis

E. Davis

W. Nye Jr.
W. Nye
C. C. Nye
A. Nye
Silas Lawrence
Saml. Lawrence
Mrs. Lewis
F. P. Stadley

A. M. Staverich
R. Bourne
Town House
Adams Shop
& Old Fellows Hall
Late Academy G. E. Clark Principal

R. Bourne
Swift

Mrs. Lewis
H. F. Fish, occp. by W. Hewins
B. Dimmick
R. Bourne
J. D. Lewis
C. Dimmick
Jos. Lawrence

G. W. Donaldson
J. McLane
Town Farm
S. Bourne

Crockery Pond

N. Robinson

E. Butler
O. C. Swift
G. W. Swift
T. L. Swift
Mrs. E. Swift

A. Mitchell
A. Nye
O. Goodspeed

T. Nye
J. Swift Pond
P. Nye
S. Davis Est.
Mrs. Parker

Mrs. Sampson
W. Edwards

O. P. Robinson
D. Davis
H. Goodspeed

P. Grant
E. Luce

Mrs. Butler

E. Butler

Mrs. Hatch
School
B. Pinney
B. P. Hatch
Store P. O.
Mrs. Davis
Neck Parish

Mrs. Davis Store
H. Southwick

S. E. Swift
R. Robinson
Store Est.
B. S. Shop
W. Davis 2nd.
S. J. Bourne

Schgolt
Store
B. Robinson

S. Hatch

E. Hatch
B. Holmes
E. Butler
J. G. Jones

Cemetery   Fresh Pond

J. R. Lawrence

A. Gifford

J. Lawrence
S. H. Hamblin

S. Hatch
B. P. Swift

FALMOUTH LANDING

Bowman's Pond

D. B. Hatch
J. Fish
B. Dimmick
F. Davis
N. Davis
J. Fish
O. C. Swift
B. C. Gifford

J. Weeks
F. W. Luce
G. W. Fish
H. Fish
P. Landers
Store House

Salt
Pond

VINEYARD SOUND

37

Hog Island Harbor

Crooked Pond

WEST FALMOUTH

Wind Mill
P.O.& Union Store

Store

F A L M

Shallow Pond

Z. Cha

Jenkins Pond

Mares Pond

Woolen M

B. Swift

Spectacle Pond

J. Gifford
W. & D.E.Gifford

B. Bowerman

Long Pond

E. Lumbert

Woolen M
Mrs Cummin

J.H. Weeks

School

A Clar

M & A Gifford

R. C. Gifford

Crews Pond

J. Robinson

P. G. Moore

W Davis

T. R. Lawrence
S. W. Robinson

H. Fish

B. Hamblin

R.L. Swift

M. Robinson

Mrs Hatch

S. A. Lawrence

W. Lawrence

Cemetery
R. E. Swift

Mrs Fish

A Green

H. Lawrence

Gunning Point

D. I. Sanford

S. Lothrop
D. Lawrence

O. A. Butler

Mrs. Fish
Mrs Robinson

B. Green

T. Jones

FALMOUTH VILLAGE

J. Dimmick
N. Davis

E. Davis

O. Weeks

F. Sherman

E. Luce
J. G. Jones

Fresh Pond

FALMOUTH LANDING

Great Pond

S.P. Davis

Z. Robinson
S. Davis

Salt Pond

Bowmans Pond

Little Pond

S. Hammond
S. Chadwick

W. Eldred

School
W. Lumbert
T. Fish
J. S. Chadwick

Racing Beach

Quamquissett Harbor

T. Fish

Oyster Pond

F. Davis
W. Davis
J. Davis

W. G. Robinson

GREAT
HARBOR

BUOY
BUOY

WOODS HOLE

Long Neck

BUOY

Episcopal Ch.

BUOY

Middle Ledge
Bone Rock
Dry Ledge

BUOY
Little
Harbor

Nobska Light

BUOY
R. No 2

Ridley Harbor
Pine Island

Mink Point

38

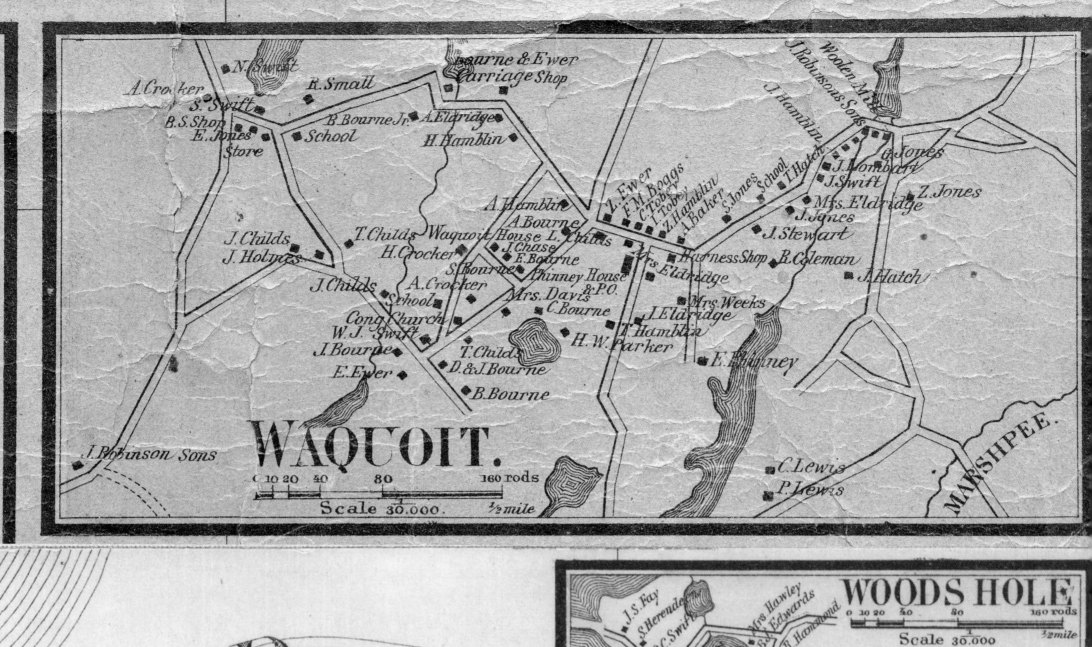

WAQUOIT.

A. Crocker
S. Swift
B.S. Shop
E. Jones
Store
N. Swift
R. Small
B. Bourne Jr.
School
A. Eldridge
H. Hamblin
Bourne & Ewer
Carriage Shop

J. Childs
J. Holmes
T. Childs
H. Crocker
Waquoit
House
A. Hamblin
A. Bourne
L. Childs
J. Chase
E. Bourne

J. Childs
A. Crocker
School
S. Bourne
Thinney House
& P.O.
Mrs. Davis
C. Bourne

Cong. Church
W. J. Swift
J. Bourne
E. Ewer
T. Childs
D. & J. Bourne
B. Bourne

Z. Ewer
F. M. Boggs
C. Tobey
T. Tobey
Z. Hamblin
A. Baker
S. Jones
School
T. Hatch
J. Lombart
J. Swift
Mrs. Eldridge
J. Jones
J. Stewart
Z. Jones

Mrs. Eldridge
Harness Shop
Mrs. Weeks
J. Eldridge
T. Hamblin
H. W. Parker
E. Finney
R. Coleman
J. Hatch

J. Robinson Sons

J. Hamblin
J. Robinsons Sons
Woolen Mill
G. Jones

C. Lewis
P. Lewis

MARSHPEE.

Scale 30.000. 0 10 20 40 80 160 rods ½ mile

N D

WOODS HOLE

J. S. Fay
S. Herendee
O. C. Swift
Mrs. Hawley
E. K. Edwards
R. Hammond

B. G. Gifford
Store House
Old Fish Market
Elm House
T. G. Davis
J. Gardner
Mrs. Bradley
S. Eldridge
Davis Est.
C. G. Bearse
J. S. Fay

J. S. Hatch
J. Webster Hotel
Nye Est.
Swift Est.
W. Davis
Butler's Est.
Fields Est.
E. Fish
W. Finney
T. Hinkley
S. F. Hamlin
R. Hamlin
Episcopal Church
Davis & Eldridge Store

Little Harbor
H. E. Sergant

Scale 30.000 0 10 20 40 80 160 rods ½ mile

West Chop
West Chop Light
O. C. West
BUOY
Rock
Low Point
Rock
Rocks
Nobska Light

e Ground

40

B. Claghorn
P. Horton
J. Claghorn
T. Daggett
A. West
B. Claghorn
C. Daggett Est.

HOLMES HOLE.
East Chop

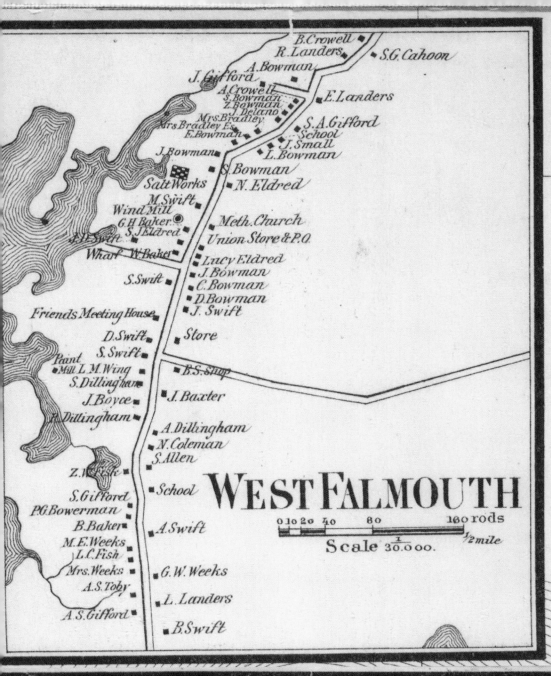

WEST FALMOUTH

B. Crowell
R. Landers
S. G. Cahoon
A. Bowman
J. Gifford
A. Crowell
E. Landers
S. Bowman
Z. Bowman
Z. Delano
Mrs. Bradley Es.
S. A. Gifford
E. Bowman
School
J. Small
J. Bowman
L. Bowman
S. Bowman
M. Swift
N. Eldred
Salt Works
Wind Mill
G. H. Baker
Meth. Church
S. J. Eldred
Union Store & P.O.
J. D. Swin
W. Baker
Wharf
Lucy Eldred
J. Bowman
S. Swift
C. Bowman
D. Bowman
J. Swift
Friends Meeting House
D. Swift
Store
S. Swift
Paint
Mill L. M. Wing
B. S. Shop
S. Dillingham
J. Boyce
J. Baxter
R. Dillingham
A. Dillingham
N. Coleman
S. Allen
Z. W. Fish
School
S. Gifford
P. G. Bowerman
B. Baker
A. Swift
M. E. Weeks
L. C. Fish
Mrs. Weeks
G. W. Weeks
A. S. Toby
L. Landers
A. S. Gifford
B. Swift

Scale 1/30.000.
0 10 20   40   80   160 rods   1/2 mile

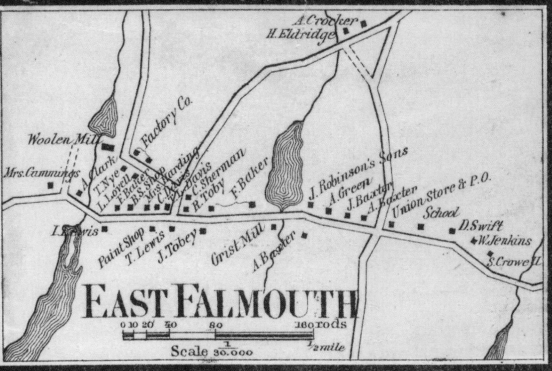

EAST FALMOUTH

A. Crocker
H. Eldridge
Factory Co.
Woolen Mill
A. Clark
Mrs. Cummings
T. Nye
L. Lovell
F. Baxter
Mrs. Harding
B. S. Shop
C. Davis
C. Sherman
R. Toby
F. Baker
J. Robinson's Sons
A. Green
J. Baxter
A. Baxter
Union Store & P.O.
School
J. Lewis
Paint Shop
T. Lewis
J. Tobey
Grist Mill
A. Baxter
D. Swift
W. Jenkins
S. Crowell

Scale 1/30.000.
0 10 20 40   80   160 rods   1/2 mile

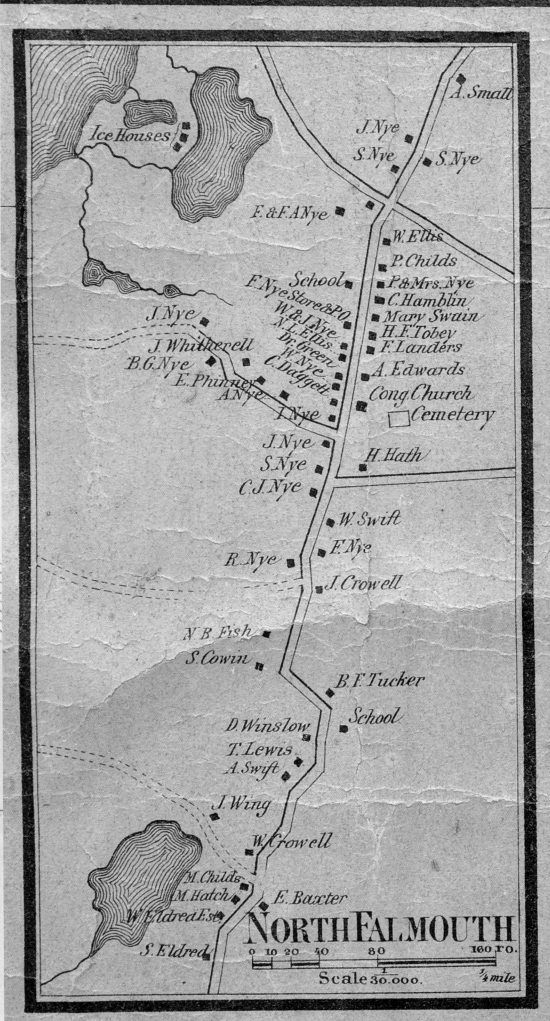

NORTH FALMOUTH

A. Small
Ice Houses
J. Nye
S. Nye
S. Nye
F. & F. A. Nye
W. Ellis
P. Childs
School
P. & Mrs. Nye
J. Nye
F. Nye Store & P.O.
C. Hamblin
W. & J. Nye
Mary Swain
J. Whitherell
N. L. Ellis
H. F. Tobey
B. G. Nye
Dr. Green
F. Landers
E. Phinney
W. Nye
A. Nye
C. Daggett
A. Edwards
J. Nye
Cong. Church
J. Nye
Cemetery
S. Nye
H. Hath
C. J. Nye
W. Swift
F. Nye
R. Nye
J. Crowell
N. B. Fish
S. Cowin
B. F. Tucker
School
D. Winslow
T. Lewis
A. Swift
J. Wing
W. Crowell
M. Childs
M. Hatch
E. Baxter
W. Eldred Est.
S. Eldred

Scale 1/30.000.
0 10 20 40   80   160 ro.   1/4 mile

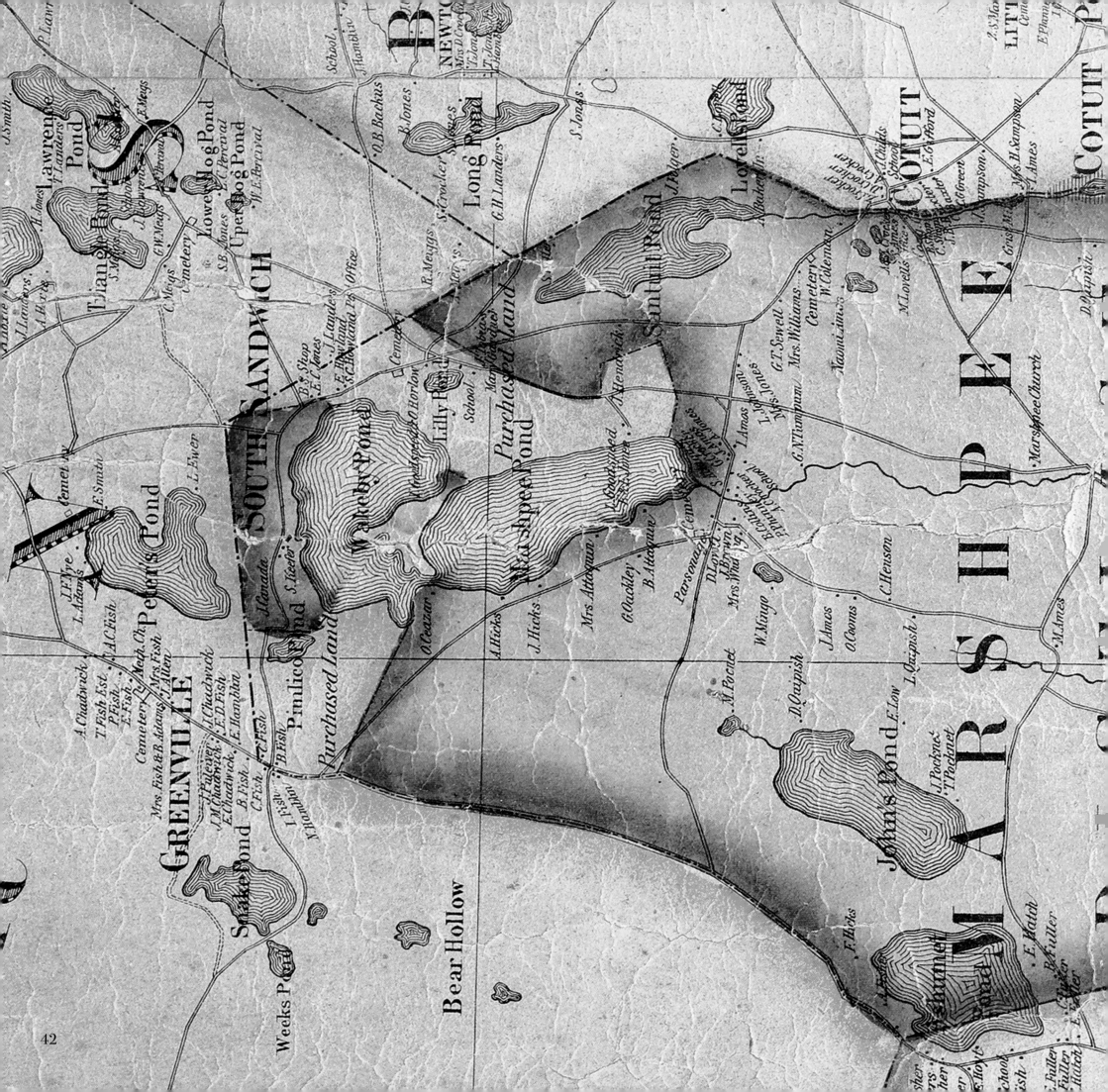

High Ground

Little

Neck

Great Neck

T
H

AQUOIT VILLAGE

Succonesset Shoal

BUOY

Succonesset

Waquoit Bay

W.H.Sampson.

Mrs.I.Nickerson.
D.Bagers.
J.Lamburt.
I.Adams.

A.Hoter.
S.Godfrey.
E.Nesmet.

W.H.Howland.
N.S.Pocknet.
S.Cooper.
L.Jackson.

School.
D.Mia.
E.Degrass J.Squibb.
C.Degrass.

J.Wilber.

J.Weequish.

T.Jonah.
P.Lewis.

R.Gardner.

J.Gardners Est.

Z.Jones.
J.Hatch.

C.Lewis.

P.Lewis.

Store House.

E.E.Weber.
B.Bourne.

U.Childs.

Hambly Pond

Quasnet River

Tober

Moronscoy Island

Bay

River

Childs

Marine
Railing

S.Boun.
S.Bourne.

Hatch
Hockley

43

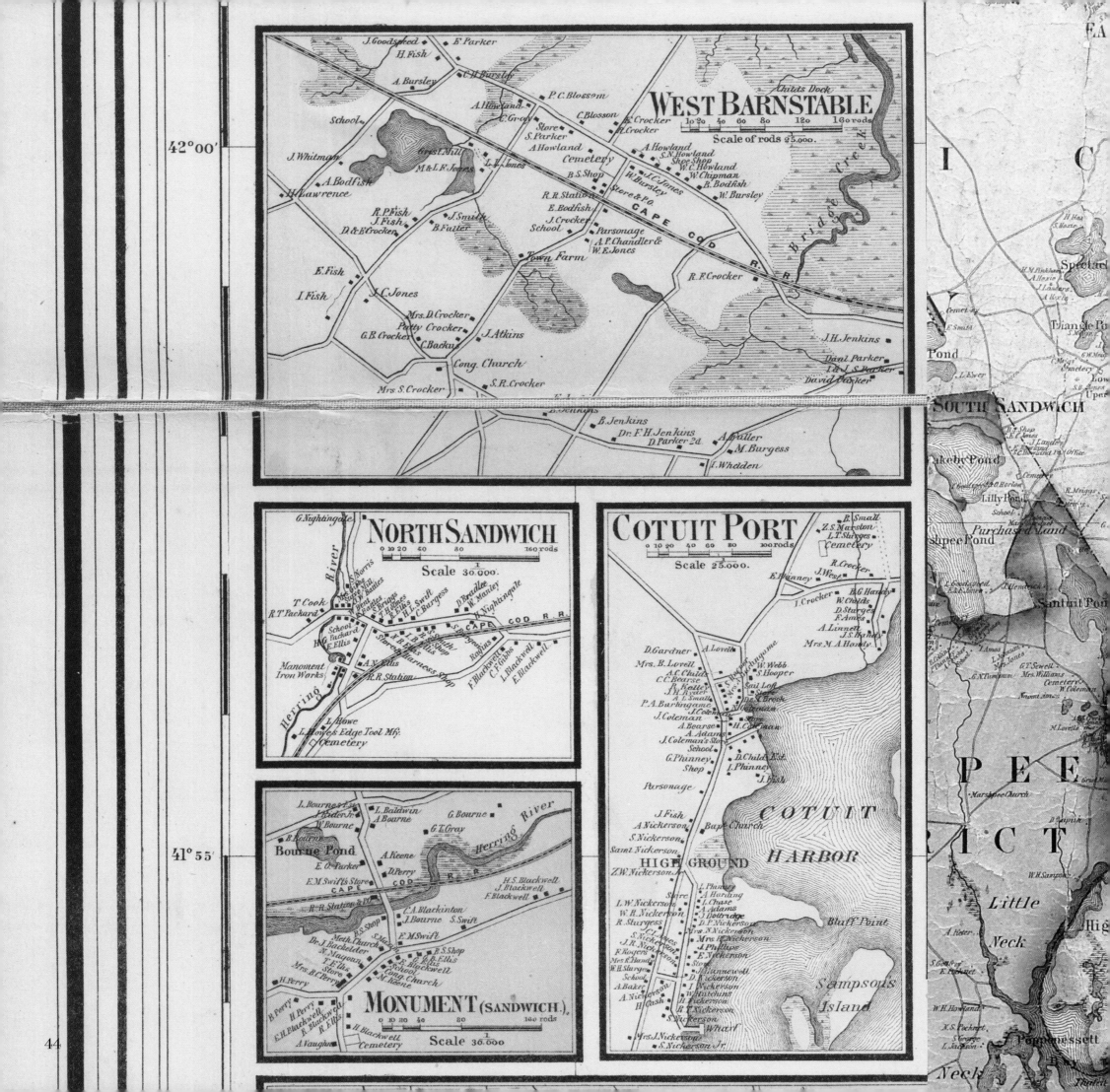

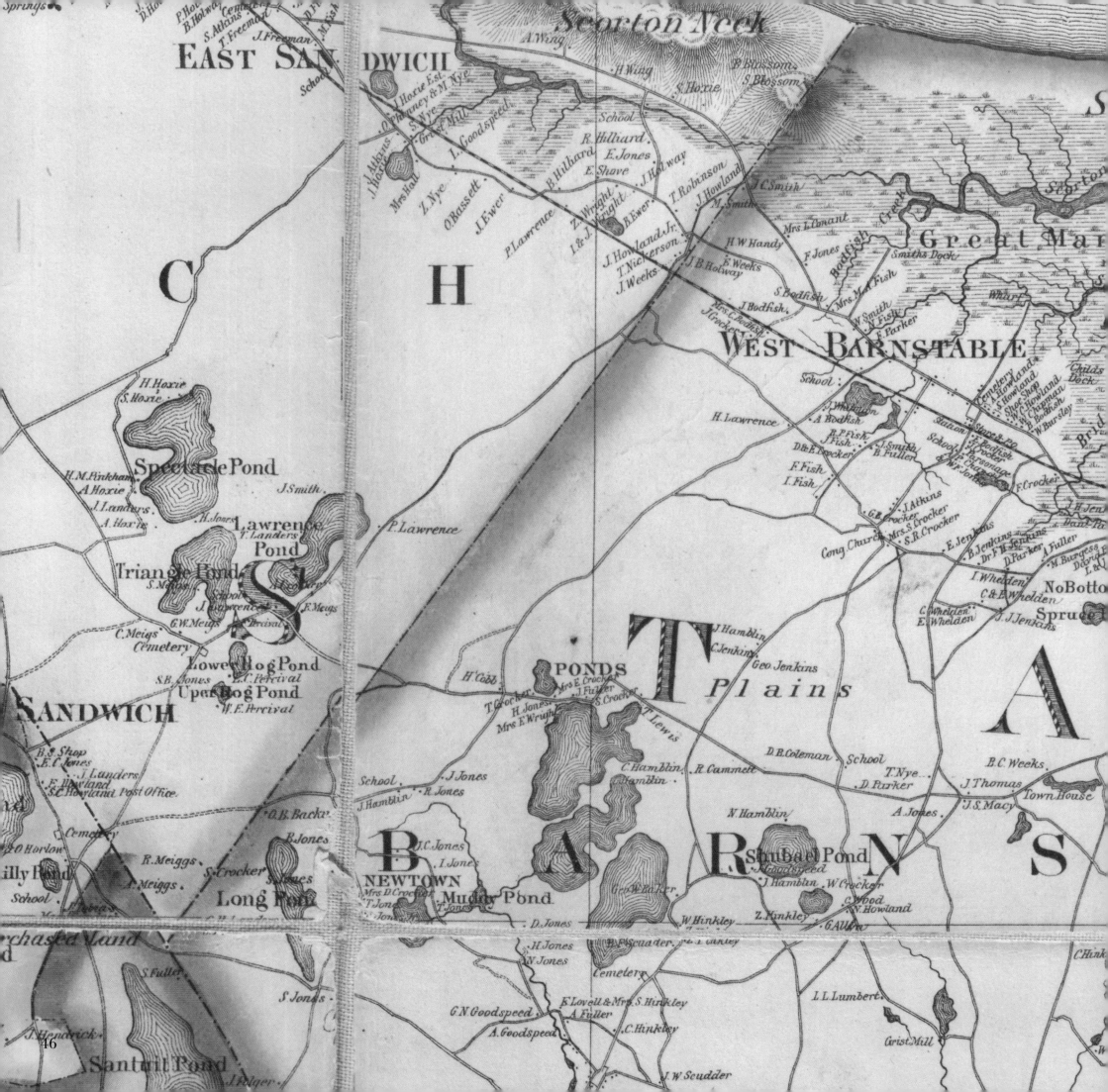

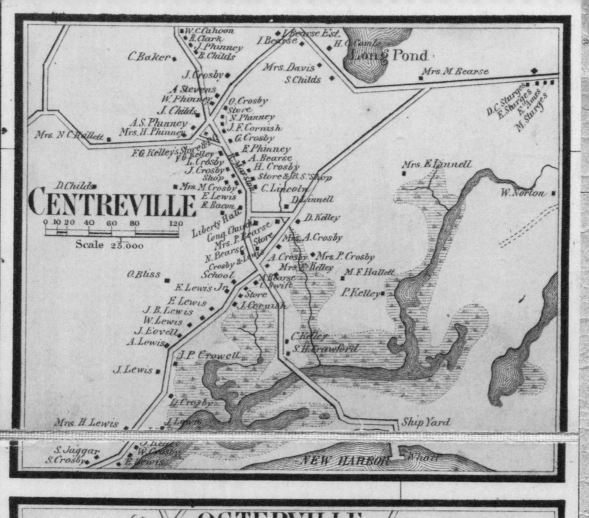
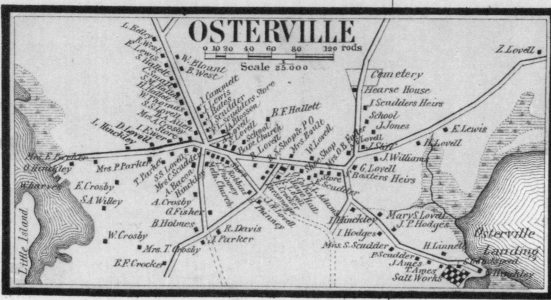
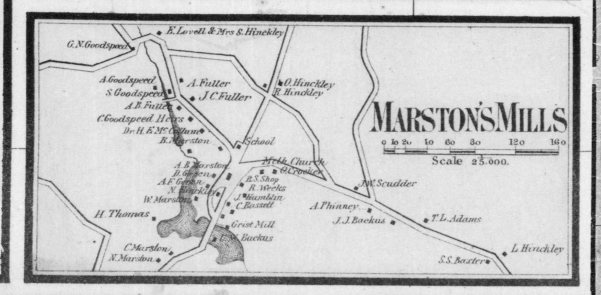

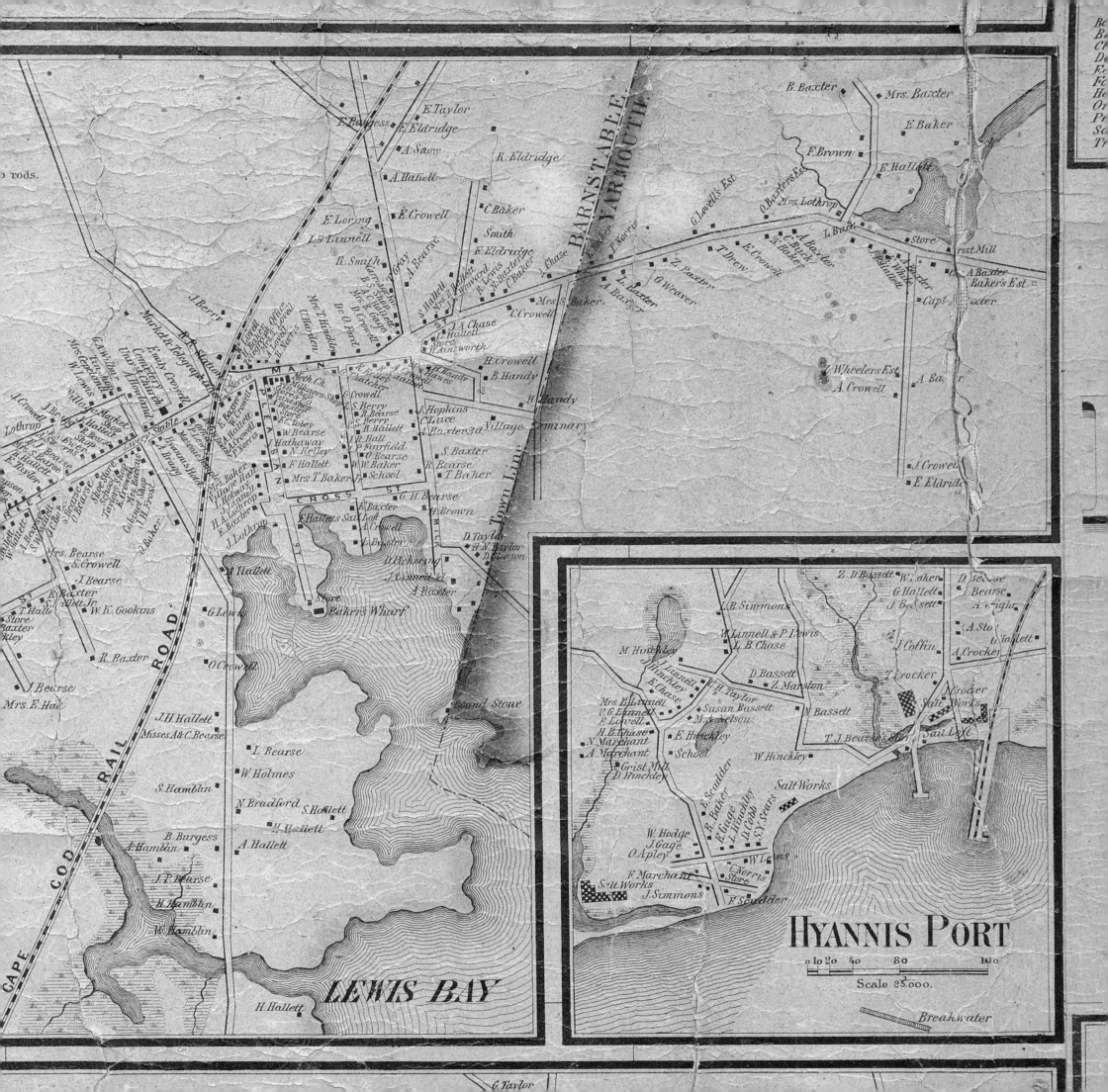

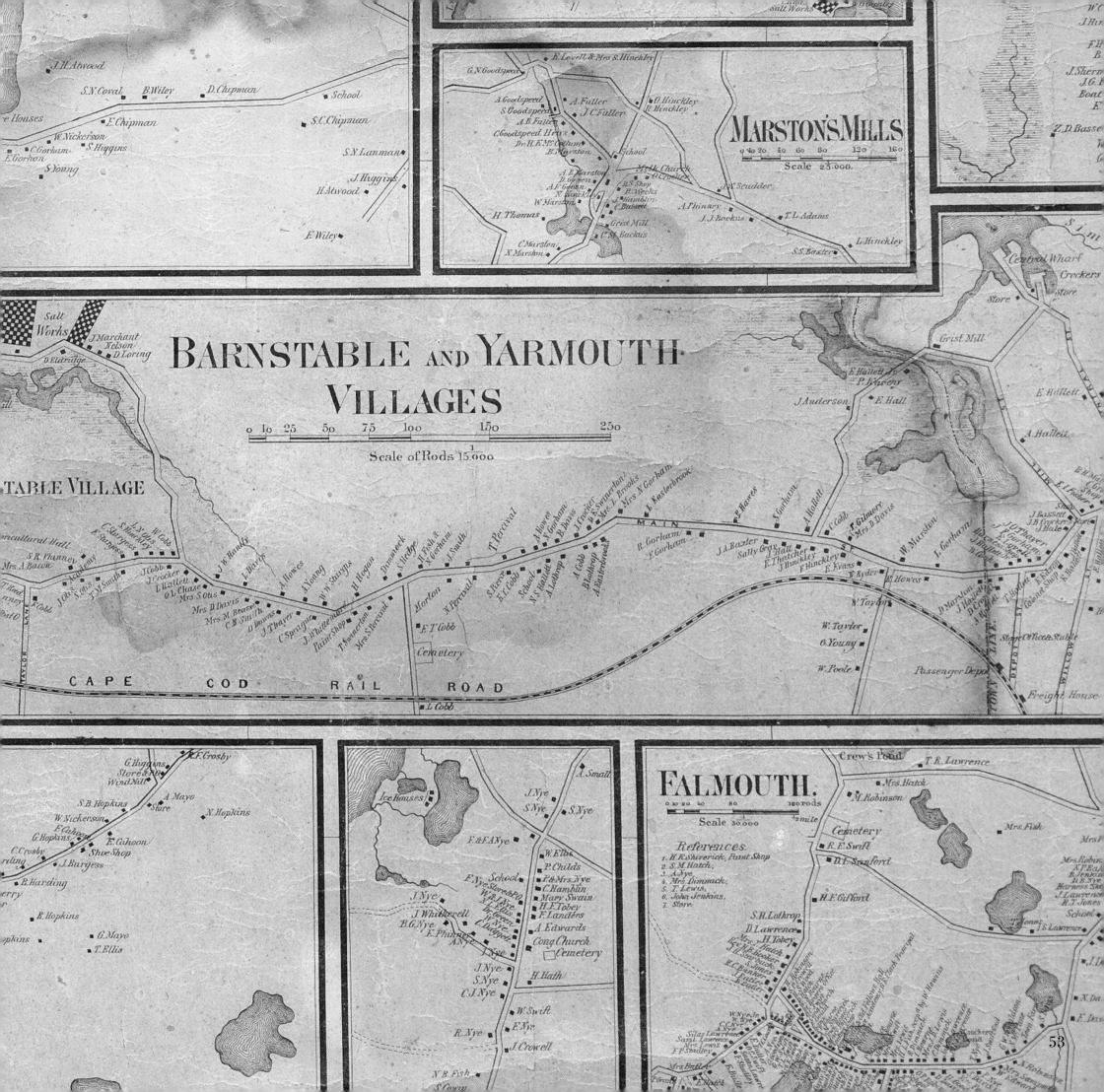

MARSTON'S MILLS

Scale 25.000

J.H.Atwood
S.N.Coval   B.Wiley   D.Chipman   School
e Houses
W.Nickerson   E.Chipman   S.C.Chipman
C.Gorham   S.Higgins
S.Young   S.N.Lanman
H.Atwood   J.Huggins
E.Wiley

G.N.Goodspeed   E.Lovell & Mrs S.Hinckley
A.Goodspeed   A.Fuller   O.Hinckley
S.Goodspeed   J.C.Fuller   R.Hinckley
A.B.Fuller
C.Goodspeed Heirs
Dr.H.E.M Collum   School
B.Marston
A.B.Marston   Meth Church
D.Gorsen   N.S.Shop
A.F.Gorsen   N.Hamblin   J.W.Scudder
N.Hinckley   R.Weeks
W.Marston   C.Bassett
H.Thomas   A.Phinney   J.J.Backus   T.L.Adams
Grist Mill
C.Marston   C.M.Backus
N.Marston   S.S.Baxter   L.Hinckley

BARNSTABLE AND YARMOUTH VILLAGES

Scale of Rods 15.000

o   10   25   50   75   100   150   250

Salt Works
J.Marchant
Nelson   D.Loring
D.Eldridge

Central Wharf
Crockers
Store   Store
Grist Mill
E.Hallett Jr   P.Vincent
J.Anderson   E.Hall   E.Hallett
A.Hallett

STABLE VILLAGE

Agricultural Hall
L.N.Otis   S.Hackley   W.Cobb
E.Sturgess   J.W.Hanly   J.Davis   A.Howes   Y.Young   W.W.Sturgs   H.Hogan   Dimmock   C.Sledge   H.Fish & Gorham   N.Smith   T.Percival   J.Howes   A.Gorham   A.Crocker   D.S.Swinerton   Mrs.J.Brooks   Mrs.N.Gorham   R.Hayes   S.Gorham   A.Hallett   C.Cobb   C.Gilmor   Mrs.D.Davis   W.Marston   L.Gorham   J.O.Thayer
Academy   S.R.Phinney   J.Cobb   J.Crocker   L.Hallett   O.L.Chase   Mrs.S.Otis   A.Young   S.Pierce   E.L.Cobb   School   N.S.Hallett   A.Lothrop   A.Cobb   Blackrop   R.Gorham   E.Gorham   J.A.Baxler   Sally Gray   J.Hall   F.Thatcher   J.Hinckley   F.Hinckley   E.Evans   W.Ryder   E.Howes
T.M.Smith   Mrs.M.Bearse   C.B.Smith   D.Downs   Morton   N.Percival   Mrs.A.Eastabrook   W.Taylor   D.Marston
J.Thayer   C.Sprague   J.Whiteman   Paint Shop   T.Swinerton   Mrs.N.Percival   E.T.Cobb   W.Taylor   G.Young
Cemetery   W.Poole   Passenger Depot

CAPE   COD   RAIL   ROAD
L.Cobb   Freight House

F.Crosby
G.Higgins
Store & P.O   A.Mayo
Wind Mill   Store   N.Hopkins
S.B.Hopkins
W.Nickerson   E.Cahoon   Shoe Shop
F.Cahoon
G.Hopkins
C.Crosby   J.Burgess
R.Harding
R.Hopkins   G.Mayo
pkins   T.Ellis

Ice Houses
J.Nye   A.Small
S.Nye   S.Nye
F. & F.A.Nye
W.Ellis
P.Childs
F.Nye Store&P.O   P.&Mrs.Nye
School   C.Hamblin
W.B.Nye   Mary Swain
W.Ellis   H.F.Tobey
F.Landers
J.Nye   B.Green   A.Edwards
J.Whitorell   E.Lidgett   Cong.Church
B.G.Nye   A.Nye   Cemetery
E.Phinney
J.Nye
S.Nye   H.Hath
C.J.Nye
W.Swift
R.Nye   F.Nye
N.B.Fish   J.Crowell
S.Corn

FALMOUTH.

Scale 30.000

o   10   20   30   ½ mile   100 rods

References.
1. H.E.Shiverick, Paint Shop
2. S.M.Hatch
3. A.Nye
4. Mrs.Dimmick,
5. T.Lewis
6. John Jenkins,
7. Store

Crew's Pond   T.R.Lawrence
Mrs.Hatch
M.Robinson
Cemetery   Mrs.Fish
R.E.Swift
D.L.Sanford
H.F.Gifford
S.H.Lothrop
D.Lawrence
H.Tobey   Mrs.Hatch

53

SOUTH DENNIS & WEST H

Scale of Rods 30,000

0 25 50 100 150 200 250

SOUTH YARMOUTH

WEST DENNIS

WEST YARMOUTH

Parkers Neck

Dog Fish Shoal

Swan Pond

Flax Pond

Plashes

Lewis Pond

Parker Pond

School

Salt Works

LEWIS BAY

Point Cammon

Gazelle Rock

Senator Shoal

North Channel

N.W. 3/4 W.

PASS RIVER

O. Baxter
R. Baxter
L. T. Thatcher
Paint Shop
G. Nickerson
S. Baker
O. Vickerson Jr.
O. Harden
P. Hayden
Mrs. A. Bangs
H. Bangs
A. Bangs
G. E. V. Boren
F. P. Rogers
S. Rogers
S. Nickerson
M. B. Nickerson
L. Baker
J. Baker
J. Nickerson
J. Nickerson
O. Baker
B. Baker
A. Studley
Mrs. F. Chase
H. G. Alexander

Cemetery

55

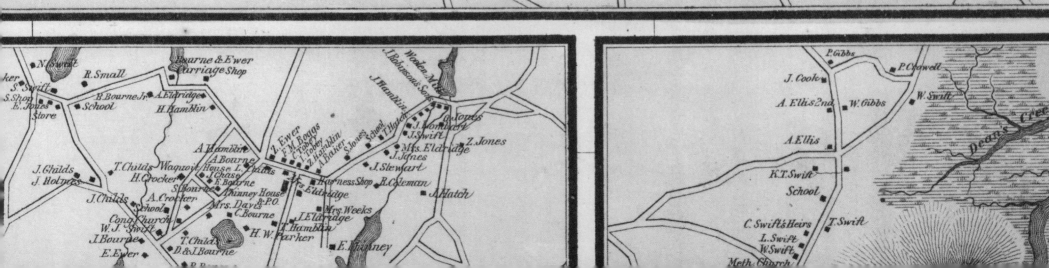

Kill Pond Bar

Fish Shoal

Dog

SOUTH DENNIS & WEST HARWICH.

Scale of Rods 30,000

SOUTH DENNIS

SOUTH DENNIS

WEST DENNIS

SOUTH YARMOUTH

WEST YARMOUTH

Parkers Neck

BASS RIVER

Long Pond

Swan Pond

Germans Hill 138 Ft.

Halfway Pond

Plashes

Swan Pond

Lewis Pond

Grand Isle

59.

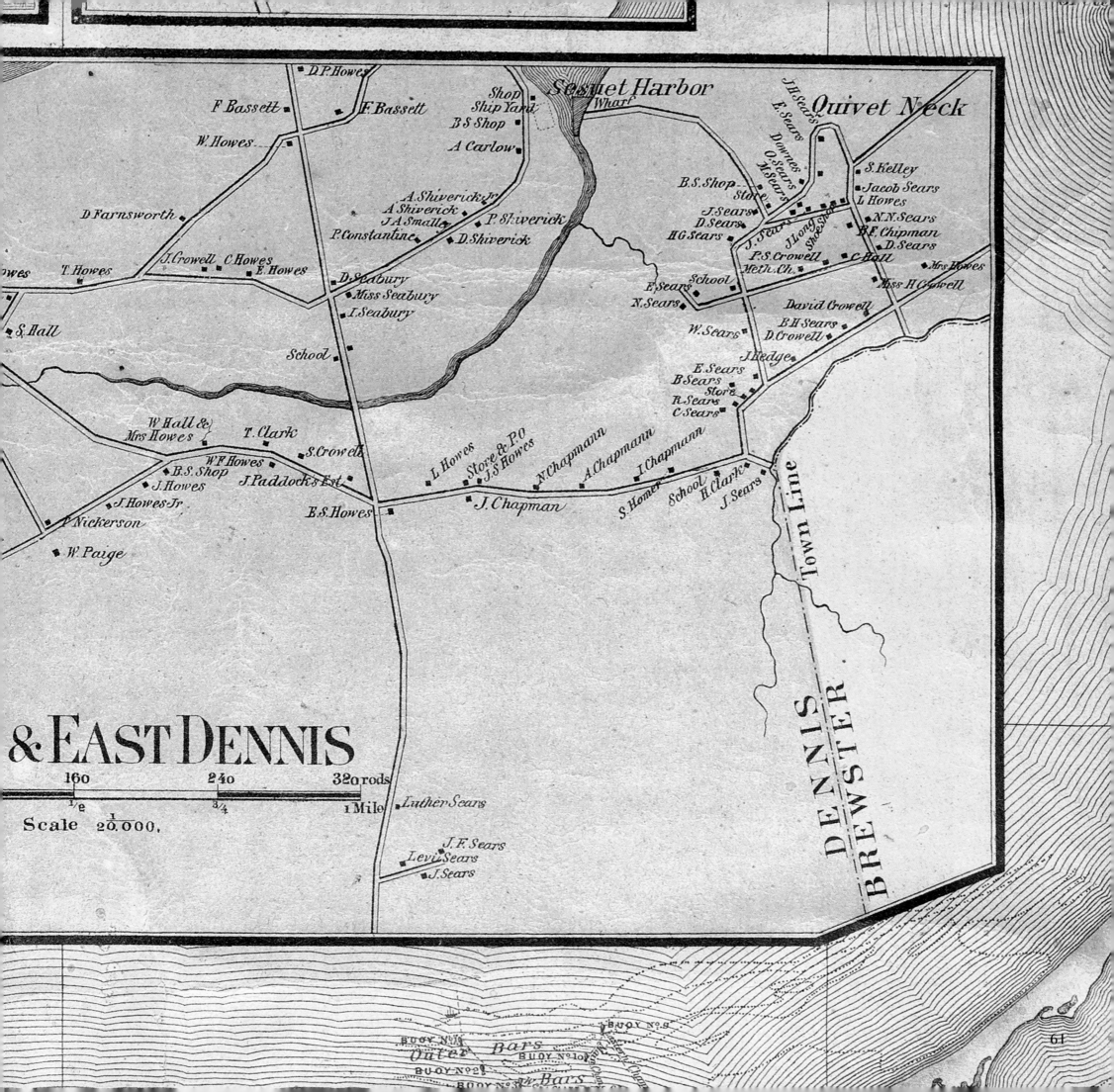

Sesuet Harbor

Quivet Neck

D.P.Howes

F Bassett   E.Bassett   Shop
                                      Ship Yard   Wharf
W.Howes   B S Shop
                                       A Carlow   J.Sears
                                                                  E.Sears
                                                          B.S.Shop   S.Kelley
D Farnsworth   A.Shiverick Jr.   Downes   Store   Jacob Sears
                               A Shiverick   O Sears   M.Sears   L Howes
                    J A Smaller   P Shiverick   J.Sears   N.N.Sears
          T.Howes   P.Constantine   D.Shiverick   D.Sears   J.Sears   B.F.Chipman
owes   J.Crowell C.Howes   H.G Sears   J.Long Shp D.Sears
                    E.Howes   J.Sears Shoe Shp
                    D.Seabury   P.S.Crowell   C.Hall
S.Hall   Meth.Ch.   Mrs Howes
                    Miss Seabury   E.Sears   School   Miss H Crowell
                    I.Seabury   N.Sears
                                                                           David Crowell
                                                          W.Sears   B H Sears
                    School   D.Crowell
                                                                   J.Hedge
                                                          E.Sears
          W Hall &   B Sears   Store
          Mrs Howes   T.Clark   R.Sears
                    S.Crowell   C.Sears
          W.F.Howes
          B.S.Shop   L Howes   Store & P.O   N.Chapmann   A.Chapmann   I Chapmann
          J.Howes   J.Paddock's Est.   J.S Howes   School   H.Clark
P.Nickerson J.Howes Jr   School
                    E.S.Howes   J.Chapman   S.Homer   J.Sears
W.Paige

& EAST DENNIS

160   240   320 rods
½   ¾   1 Mile
Scale 20,000.

Luther Sears

J.F.Sears

Levi Sears

J.Sears

DENNIS
BREWSTER.

Town Line

BUOY Nº 7

Outer Bars   BUOY Nº 8   BUOY Nº 9
BUOY Nº 10
BUOY Nº 2
BUOY Nº

61

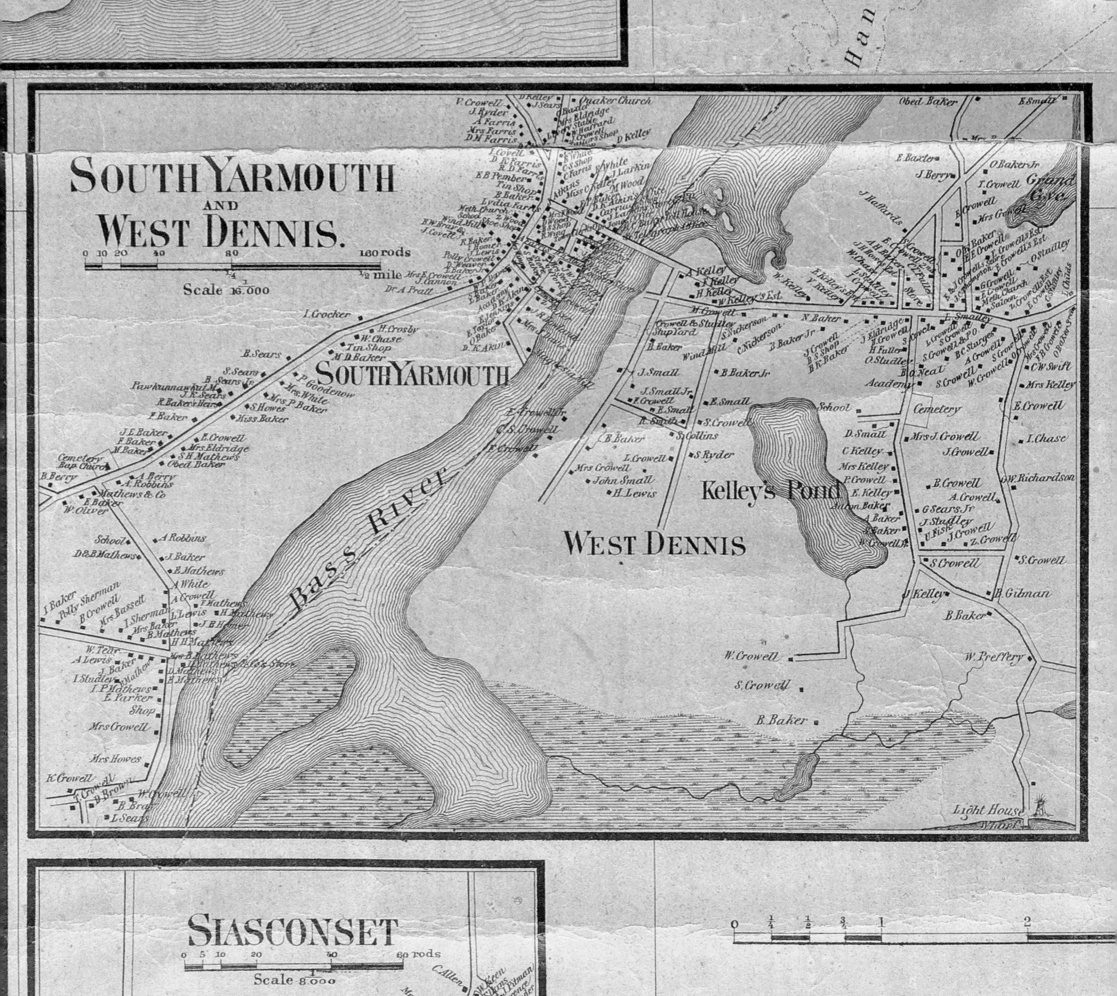

SOUTH YARMOUTH
AND
WEST DENNIS.

0 10 20 40 80 160 rods

Scale 16,000

¼   ½ mile

SOUTH YARMOUTH

WEST DENNIS

Bass River

Kelley's Pond

Grand Cove

Light House
Wharf

J. Chase's Wharf

Hand

Quaker Church

SIASCONSET

0 5 10 20 40 60 rods

Scale 8,000

School

J. Coleman

0   ¼   ½   ¾   1   2

SWASH

62

SOUTH DENNIS & WEST HARWICH

Scale of Rods 30,000

63

EAST & WEST BREWSTER
AND
BREWSTER VILLAGE.

Scale 20,000
0 10 20 40 60 80 100 150

41° 50'

BARNSTABLE BAY

Breakwater
Packet Wharf
G.E.Wetherbee
C.Small & N.N.Cha
Cobb's Pond
J.Seabury

E.Nickerson
SaltWorks   S.Rogers
E.Bevins
B.Foster
E.Higgins   S.Freeman   E.Cobb
G.Mallard
W.W.Shop
Winslow's Marble Shop
Mrs.D.Snow   Univt Church
J.Maker
Cemetery
B.Cobb
Mrs P.Lincoln   W.L.Knowles
T.Jarvis
I.Freeman
T.Crocker
B.Paine   G.Copel
Bapt.Chu
T.Foster
B.F.Berry
A.Paine
J.H.Sears   Mrs.Crowell
Shoe Shop
E.Pratt   J.C.Crosby
J.Mayo & P.O.
River
Rev.L.Walcott
E.Bangs
B.Freeman
ShoeShop   B.Foster   J.Doyle   O.O.Keiff
J.Crocker
E.Bangs
F.Bassett
Mrs.D.Bangs   F.Crosby
D.Lincoln
School   S.Baker
O.Snow   J.Freeman
Mrs.C.Rogers   E.H.Bangs
W.Freeman   Store
W.H.Lincoln
B.Brannon
W.M.Dunbar
School House Pond
I.Clark   Hall
SaltWorks
W.Clark   C.Lincoln
A.Dunbar
J.K.Cahoon
B.B.Winslow   B.Fessenden
Stoves & Tin Store   H.Bowman
E.Foster
Herring
Mrs.Clark   T.Reed   J.Bassett
J.Foster   Mrs.Smith
Store
S.Clark   S.Robbins   Z.Robbins
F.Winslow   W.H.Lee
ShoeShop
S.Doane   Mrs.Baker   J.Cro
Cemetery   A.G.Twist   J.Griffith
Mrs.M.Ruter   R.McLoud   Mrs.N.Winslow
Mrs.Carly
School   Mrs.Griffith   Mrs.O
J.Newcomb   Chadwick   A.Newcomb
Winslow   Store
Winslow   Tannery Mill   J.Rogers   C.C
Grist Mill   W.Roshins
D.Barnes   K.&W.Winslow   D.Harwood
N.Dillingham   J.McLoud   J.Newcomb   I.Berry   J.Quinby
D.Chase   J.Eldridge

64

41° 45'

L.Rogers
CAPE CO
E.Parks   Mrs.Chadbourne
W.Collins

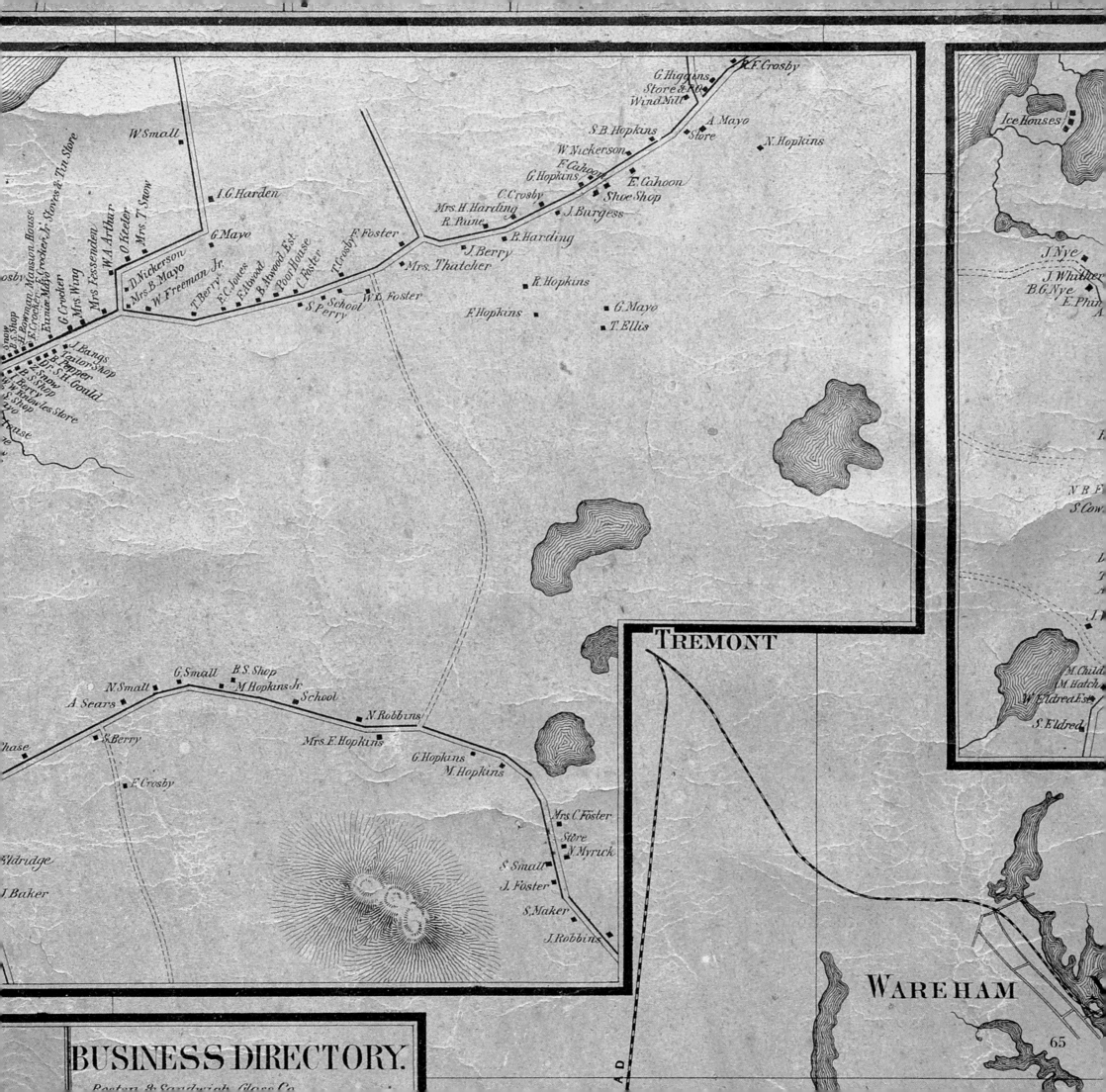

R.F. Crosby

G. Higgins
Store & P.O.
Wind Mill

W. Small

S.B. Hopkins   A. Mayo
                               Store   N. Hopkins
W. Nickerson
F. Cahoon
G. Hopkins   E. Cahoon
I.G. Harden   C. Crosby   Shoe Shop
                  Mrs. H. Harding   J. Burgess
                  R. Paine
G. Mayo   B. Harding
                  J. Berry

D. Nickerson   F. Foster
Mrs. B. Mayo   Mrs. Thatcher
W.A. Arthur   O. Keeler
Mrs. T. Snow
W. Freeman Jr. T. Crosby
Mrs Fessenden   E.C. Jones F. Atwood
Mrs Wing   T. Berry   F. Atwood R. Hopkins
G. Crocker   B. Atwood Est.
E. Crocker Jr. Stores & Tin Store   Poor House
                  C. Foster
Crosby Bowman Mansion House   W.D. Foster
E. Crocker Mayo   S. Perry School   F. Hopkins   G. Mayo
                                                         T. Ellis
B.S. Shop
J. Banqs   Tailor Shop
Z. Snow   B. Pepper
B.S. Shop   Dr. S.H. Gould
I. Berry
W. Knowles Store
S. Shop

Ice Houses

J. Nye
J. Whither
B.G. Nye
E. Phin

N R E
S. Cow

TREMONT

G. Small   B.S. Shop
N. Small   M. Hopkins Jr.
A. Sears   School
                  N. Robbins
Chase
S. Berry
                  Mrs. E. Hopkins
                       G. Hopkins
F. Crosby   M. Hopkins

M. Child
M. Hatch
W. Eldred Est
S. Eldred

Mrs. C. Foster
                  Store
                  N. Myrick

Eldridge   S. Small
J. Baker   J. Foster

                  S. Maker

                  J. Robbins

WAREHAM

65

NAMSKAKET

Namskaket Creek

Salt Works

ORLEANS

Mill Hill

O R L

EAST BREWSTER

Bakers Pond

Cliff Pond

S T E R

T

NAMEQUOIT

PORTANIMIC

PLEASANT B

67

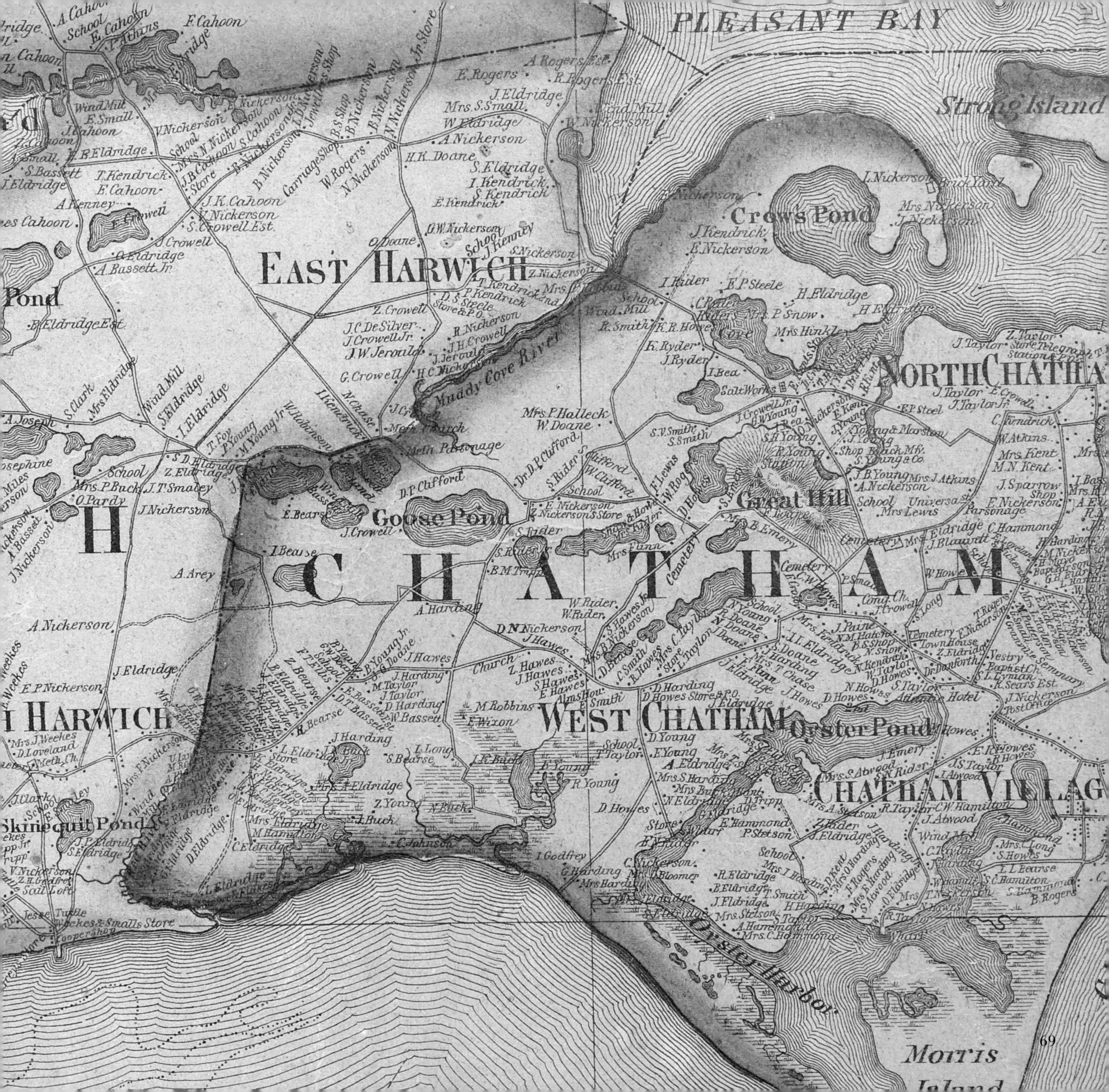
PLEASANT BAY
Strong Island
Crows Pond
Brick Yard
EAST HARWICH
Muddy Cove River
NORTH CHATHAM
Great Hill
Goose Pond
CHATHAM
WEST CHATHAM
Oyster Pond
CHATHAM VILLAG
Atlantic Hotel
Post Office
Oyster Harbor
Morris
Island
Skinequit Pond
HARWICH
Salt Works
Cemetery
Town House
Baptist Ch.
Cong. Ch.
Meth. Parsonage
School
Wind Mill
Alms Hou.

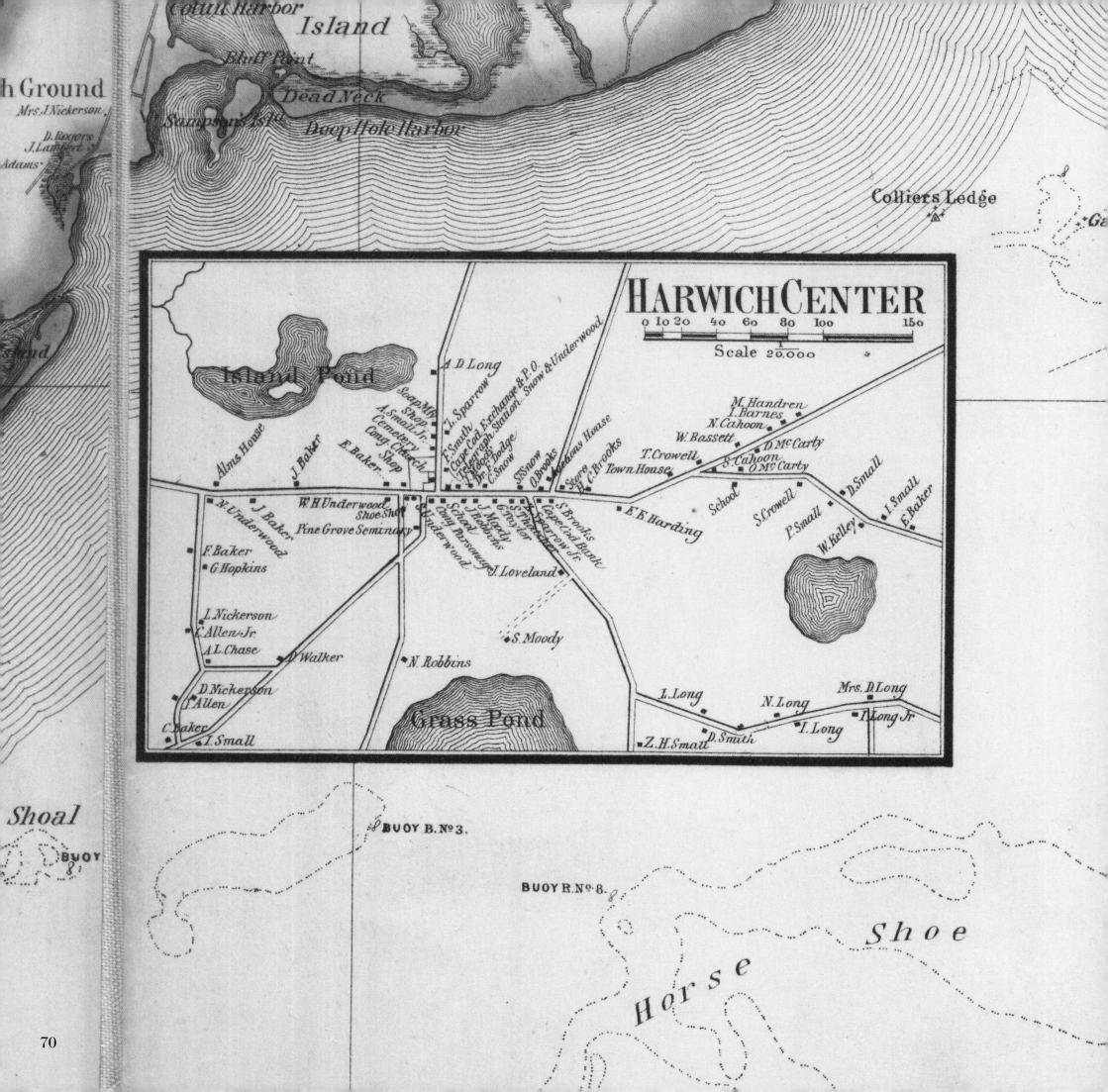

Island

Coll Harbor

Bluff Point

Dead Neck

Sampson's Isl.

Deep Hole Harbor

h Ground

Mrs. J. Nickerson

D. Rogers

J. Lambert

Adams

Colliers Ledge

HARWICH CENTER

0 10 20 40 60 80 100   150

Scale 20,000

Island Pond

Alms House

J. Baker

E. Baker

Soap Mfr. Shop

A. Small Jr.

Cemetery

Cong. Church

Shop

T. D. Long

T. Sparrow

F. Smith

Cape Cod Exchange & P.O.

Telegraph Station

Dr. F. Dodge

T. Moody

C. Snow

Snow & Underwood

S. Snow

O. Brooks

Store

H. C. Brooks

Brekons House

M. Handren

I. Barnes

N. Cahoon

W. Bassett

T. Crowell

Town House

D. McCarty

S. Cahoon

O. McCarty

School

S. Crowell

P. Small

D. Small

I. Small

E. Baker

E. E. Harding

W. Kelley

N. Underwood

J. Baker

W. H. Underwood

Shoe Shop

Pine Grove Seminary

Underwood

School

Cong. Parsonage

J. Robbins

J. Moody

G. Taylor

S. Taylor

Cape Cod Bank

T. Sparrow Jr.

S. Brooks

F. Baker

G. Hopkins

J. Loveland

L. Nickerson

C. Allen Jr.

A. L. Chase

D. Walker

N. Robbins

S. Moody

D. Nickerson

J. Allen

C. Baker

I. Small

Grass Pond

L. Long

N. Long

Mrs. D. Long

Z. H. Small

D. Smith

I. Long

I. Long Jr.

Shoal

BUOY

BUOY B. N° 3.

BUOY R. N° 8.

Horse

Shoe

70

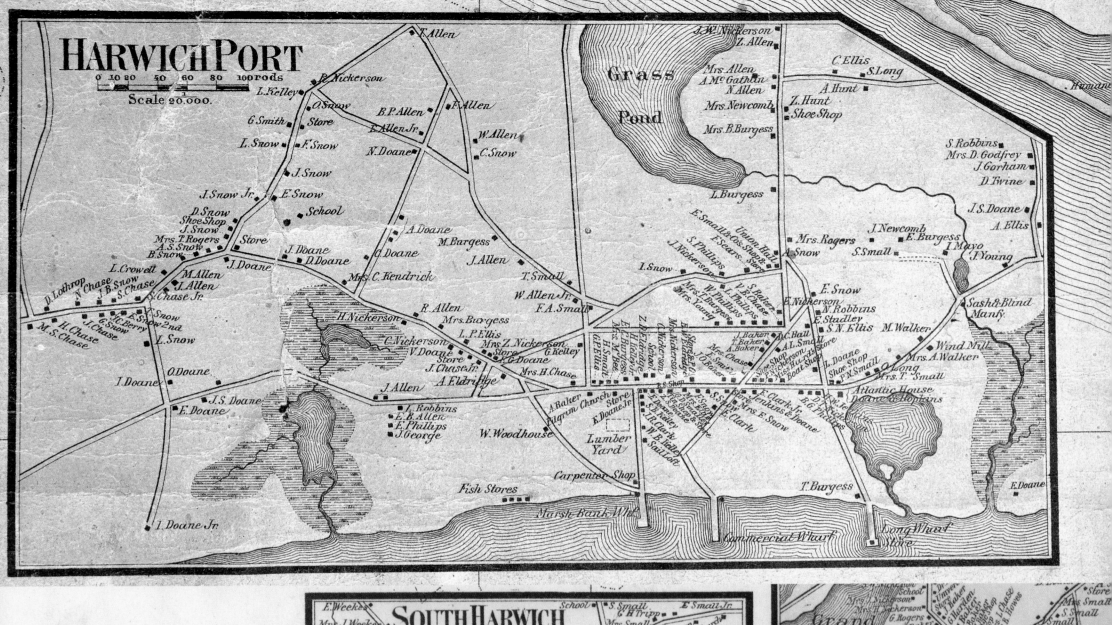

HARWICH PORT

0 10 20 40 60 80 100 rods
Scale 20.000.

T. Allen
J.W. Nickerson
Z. Allen
R. Nickerson
L. Kelley
C. Ellis
S. Long
G. Smith
O. Snow
B.P. Allen
F. Allen
Mrs. Allen
A. McGathlin
N. Allen
A. Hunt
Store
F. Allen
Z. Hunt
Shoe Shop
L. Snow
F. Snow
E. Allen Jr.
W. Allen
Mrs. Newcomb
Mrs. B. Burgess
N. Doane
C. Snow
J. Snow
S. Robbins
Mrs. D. Godfrey
J. Gorham
D. Twine
J. Snow Jr.
E. Snow
L. Burgess
D. Snow
Shoe Shop
School
J.S. Doane
J. Snow
A. Doane
E. Small & Co's Shop
T. Sears
J. Newcomb
A. Ellis
Mrs. T. Rogers
Store
A. Doane
M. Burgess
Union Hall
S. Phillips
Mrs. Rogers
E. Burgess
J. Mayo
A.S. Snow
J. Doane
C. Doane
J. Allen
J. Nickerson
A. Snow
S. Small
J. Young
B. Snow
D. Doane
I. Snow
D. Lothrop
L. Crowell
M. Allen
S. Baker
E. Snow
N. Chase
J. Allen
Store
T. Small
W. Phillips
V.R. Chase
J.B. Snow
S. Chase
Mrs. C. Kendrick
W. Allen Jr.
Mrs. T. Burgess
W. Phillips
A. Nickerson
Sash & Blind
S. Chase Jr.
R. Allen
F.A. Small
Mrs. Young
N. Robbins
Manf'y.
H. Chase
S. Snow
H. Nickerson
Mrs. Burgess
E. Stadley
O. Long
G. Berry
E. Snow 2nd
C. Nickerson
L.P. Ellis
S.N. Ellis
M. Walker
J.C. Berry
L. Snow
V. Doane
Mrs. Z. Nickerson
J. Baker
A.C. Ball
M.S. Chase
Store
Store
G. Kelley
E. Baker
A.L. Small
Wind Mill
O.C. Chase
E. Doane
Mrs. A. Walker
J. Chase Jr.
Mrs. H. Chase
Shoe Shop
J. Doane
I. Doane
O. Doane
A. Eldridge
Boat Shop
Shoe Shop
Mrs. T. Small
F.N. Small
J. Allen
Atlantic House
Doane & Hopkins
J.S. Doane
J. Robbins
A. Baker
Store
E. Doane
E. Doane
E.B. Allen
Pilgrim Church
Mrs. E. Snow
E. Phillips
E. Doane Jr.
J. George
W. Woodhouse
Lumber
Yard
T. Burgess
W.B. Kelley
Sail Loft
Carpenter Shop
Fish Stores
Marsh Bank Whf.
I. Doane Jr.
Commercial Wharf
Long Wharf
Store

Grass Pond

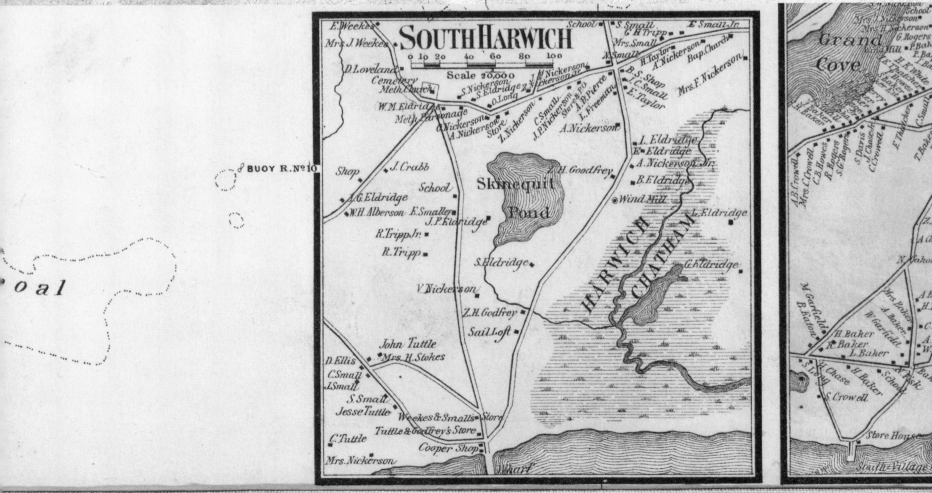

SOUTH HARWICH

0 10 20 40 60 80 100
Scale 20.000.

E. Weekes
School
S. Small
E. Small Jr.
Mrs. J. Weekes
G.H. Tripp
Mrs. Small
D. Loveland
S. Nickerson
J.W. Nickerson
H. Taylor
A. Nickerson
Bap. Church
Cemetery
Meth. Church
S. Eldridge
O. Long
B.S. Shop
S.C. Small
Mrs. F. Nickerson
W.M. Eldridge
Z. Nickerson
E. Taylor
Meth. Parsonage
A. Nickerson
Store
C. Small
J.P. Nickerson
Meth. P.O.
A.B. Pierce
J. Freeman
Shop
J. Crabb
A. Nickerson
L. Eldridge
School
E. Eldridge
A.G. Eldridge
H. Goodfrey
A. Nickerson Jr.
W.H. Alberson
E. Smalley
J.P. Eldridge
B. Eldridge
R. Tripp Jr.
Skinequit
Pond
R. Tripp
Wind Mill
V. Nickerson
L. Eldridge
S. Eldridge
HARWICH
CHATHAM
Z.H. Godfrey
Sail Loft
G. Eldridge
John Tuttle
D. Ellis
Mrs. H. Stokes
C. Small
J. Small
S. Small
Jesse Tuttle
C. Tuttle
Weekes & Smalls Store
Tuttle & Godfrey's Store
Cooper Shop
Mrs. Nickerson
Wharf

BUOY R. N°10

oal

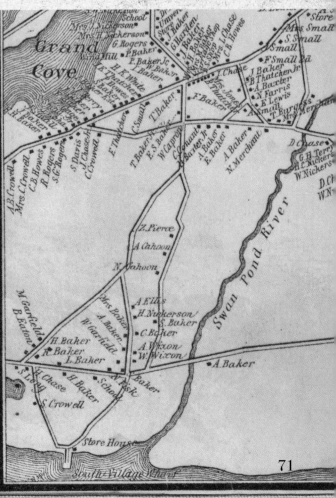

Grand
Cove

School
Mrs. J. Nickerson
Mrs. H. Nickerson
Store
Mrs. Small
G. Rogers
S. Small
P. Baker
F. Small Ed.
E. White
H.E. White
F. Baker Jr.
H.E. Baker
J. Baker
A. Baxter
N. Farris
E. Lewis
C.B. Crowell
Mrs. L.P. Crowell
C.B. Howes
S.G. Rogers
T. Baker Jr.
W. Capron
T. Baker
F. Baker
A. Baker
Mrs. T. Merchant
A. Small
T. Burgess
S. Davis
C. Crowell
E. Thacher
Barton Jr.
A. Baker
E. Baker
N. Merchant
D. Chase
G.H. Terry
W. Nickerson
D.C.W. Nick.
Z. Pierce
A. Cahoon
N. Cahoon
Swan Pond River
M. Garfield
A. Ellis
Mrs. Baker
H. Nickerson
B. Eaton
A. Baker
H. Baker
W. Garfield
C. Baker
R. Baker
A. Wixon
L. Baker
W. Wixon
A. Baker
S. Baker
E. Fisk
Chase
H. Baker
School
S. Crowell
Store House
South Village Wharf

71

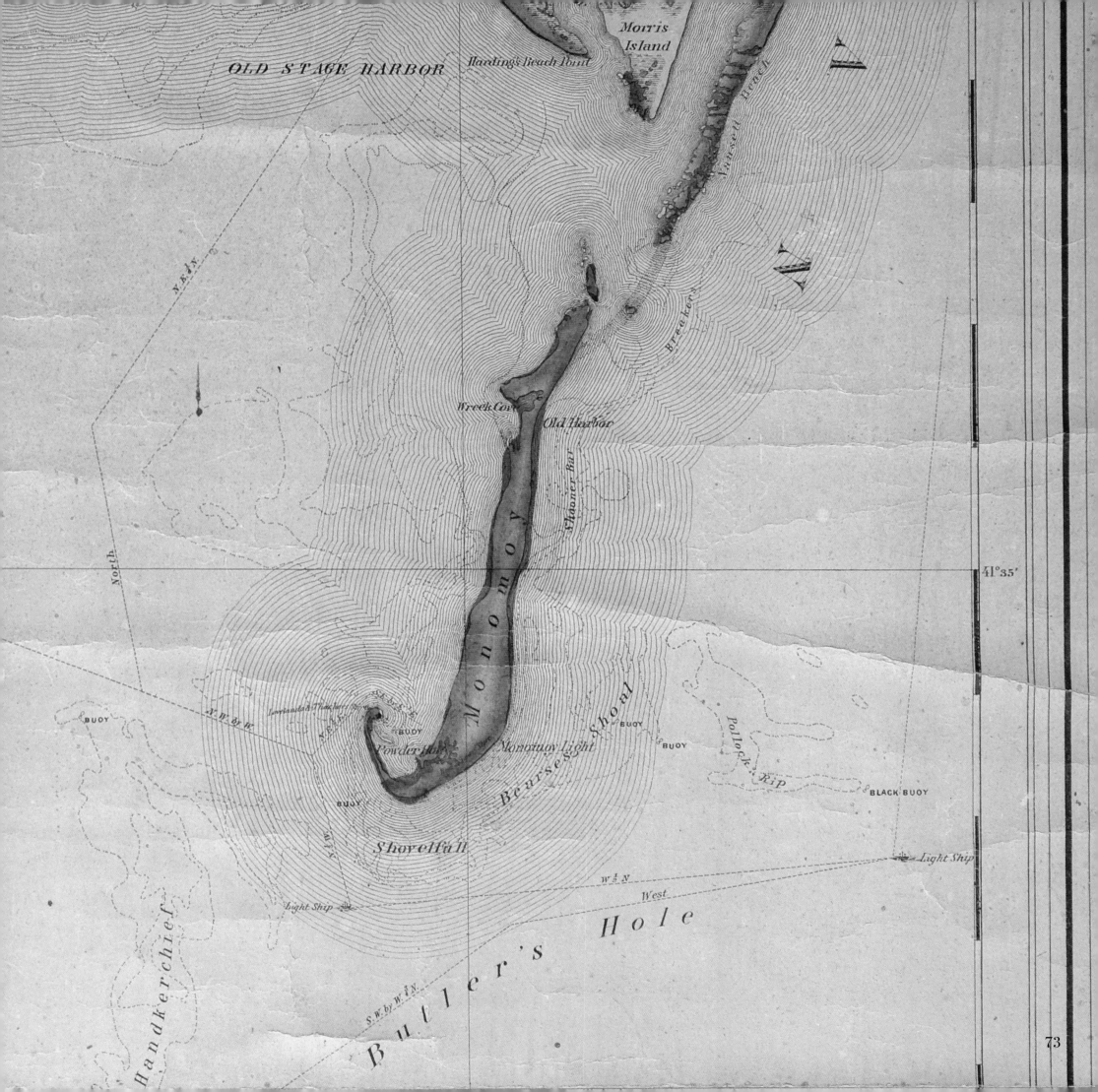

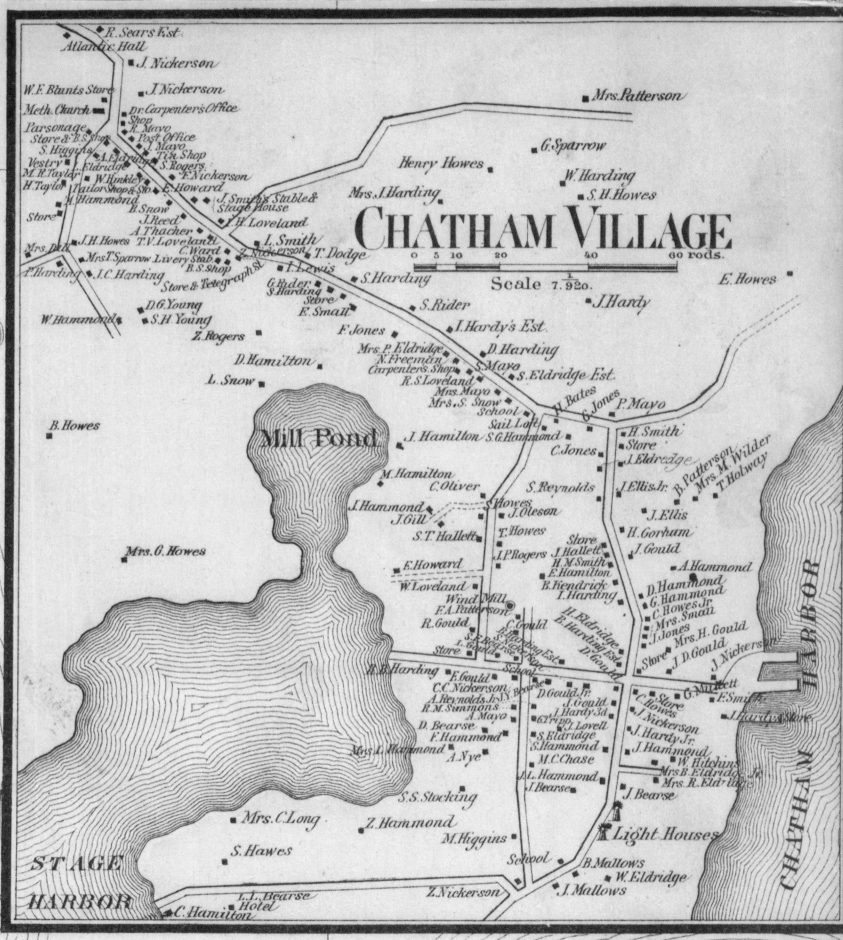

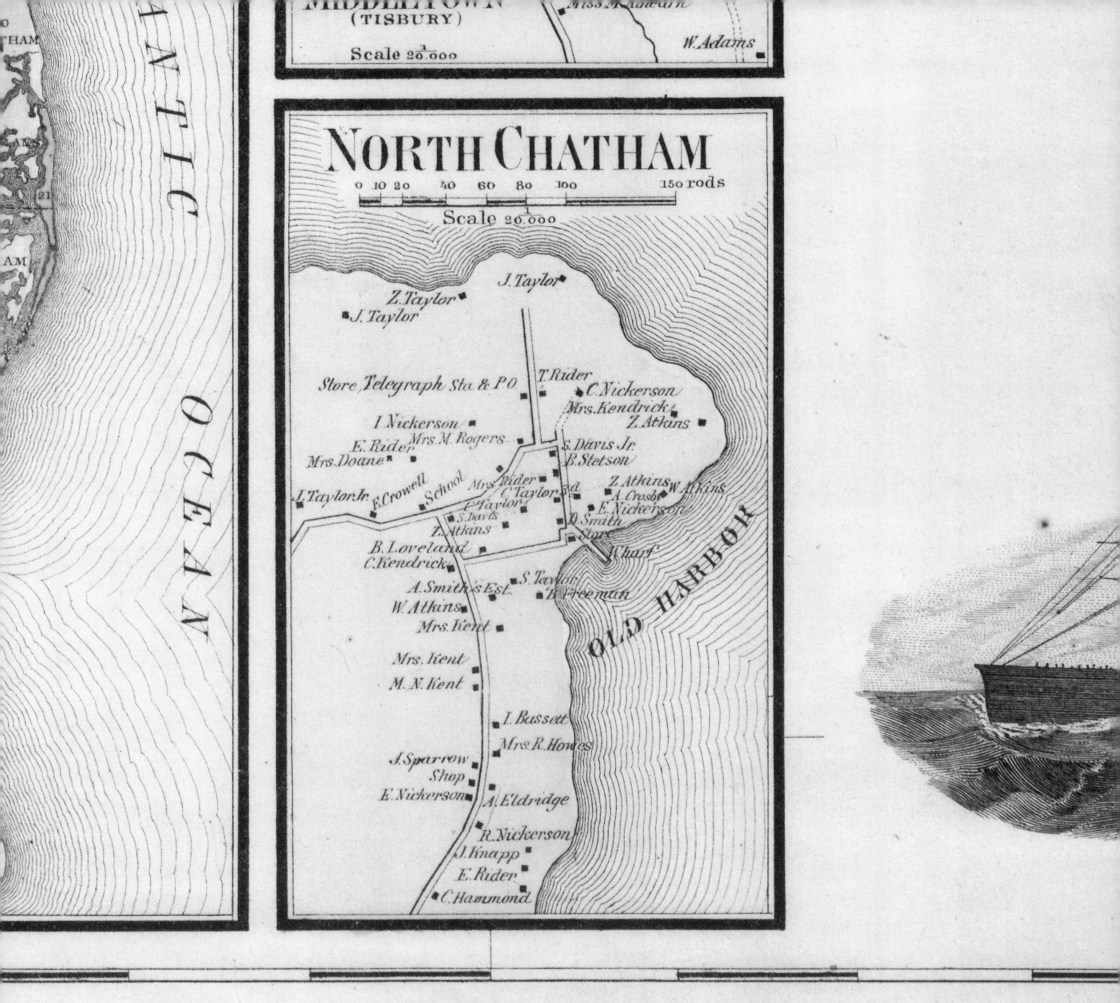

MIDDLETOWN
(TISBURY)

Miss M. Adams

Scale 20,000

W. Adams

NORTH CHATHAM

0 10 20   40   60   80 100   150 rods

Scale 20,000

ATLANTIC OCEAN

J. Taylor

Z. Taylor

J. Taylor

Store, Telegraph Sta & P.O.

T. Rider

C. Nickerson

Mrs. Kendrick

I. Nickerson

Z. Atkins

E. Rider

Mrs. M. Rogers

S. Davis Jr.

Mrs. Doane

B. Stetson

J. Taylor Jr.

E. Crowell

School

Mrs. Rider

C. Taylor 3d

Z. Atkins

W. Atkins

C. Taylor

A. Crosby

E. Nickerson

S. Davis

D. Smith

Z. Atkins

Store

B. Loveland

Wharf

C. Kendrick

A. Smith's Est.

S. Taylor

B. Freeman

W. Atkins

OLD HARBOR

Mrs. Kent

Mrs. Kent

M. N. Kent

I. Bassett

Mrs. R. Howes

J. Sparrow

Shop

E. Nickerson

A. Eldridge

R. Nickerson

J. Knapp

E. Rider

C. Hammond

70°35'

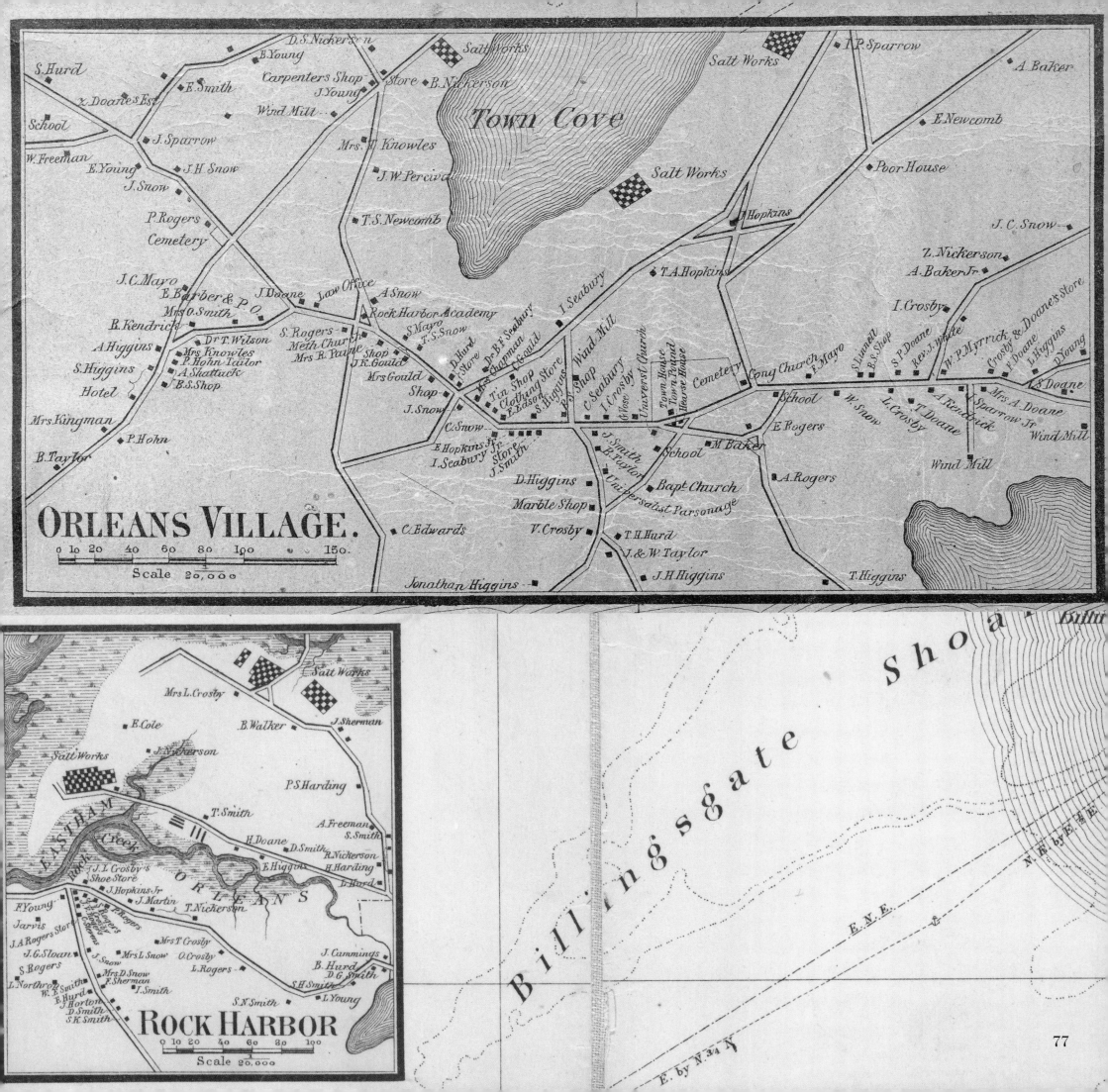

ORLEANS VILLAGE.

S. Hurd
Z. Doane's Est
School
W. Freeman
E. Young
J. Snow
P. Rogers
Cemetery
J. C. Mayo
E. Barber & P.O.
Mrs O. Smith
R. Kendrick
A. Higgins
S. Higgins
Hotel
Mrs. Kingman
B. Taylor
P. Hohn

E. Smith
J. Sparrow
J. H. Snow

D. S. Nickerson
B. Young
Carpenters Shop
J. Young
Wind Mill
Store
B. Nickerson

Salt Works

Town Cove

Salt Works

T. P. Sparrow
A. Baker

E. Newcomb

Poor House

J. Hopkins

Z. Nickerson
A. Baker Jr

I. Crosby

J. C. Snow

Mrs. T. Knowles
J. W. Percival
T. S. Newcomb

Salt Works

T. A. Hopkins

I. Seabury

J. Doane
Law Office
Rock Harbor Academy
S. Rogers
Meth. Church
Mrs R. Paine
Shop
J. K. Gould
Mrs Gould
Shop
J. Snow
C. Snow
E. Hopkins Jr
I. Seabury

A. Snow
S. Mayo
T. S. Snow
D. Hurd
Store
Dr. B. F. Seabury
J. Chapman
G. Gould

Wind Mill
P. Shop
S. Higgins
Store
J. Smith

Tin Shop
Clothing Store
E. Eason

C. Seabury
I. Crosby

Wind Mill
C. Seabury
Glass
Univers'l Church
Town House
Town Pound
Hearse House

Cemetery
Cong Church
E. Mayo
S. Linnett
B. S. Shop
S. P. Doane
Rev J. Wilde
W. P. Myrrick
Crosby & Doane's Store
P. Doane
L. Higgins
D. Young

J. S. Doane

School
W. Snow
L. Crosby
A. Rendrick
T. Doane
Sparrow Jr
Mrs A. Doane

Wind Mill

E. Rogers
M. Baker
J. Smith
B. Taylor
School
A. Rogers

Wind Mill

D. Higgins
Marble Shop
V. Crosby
T. H. Hurd
Bapt Church
Universalist Parsonage

C. Edwards
J. & W. Taylor
J. H. Higgins
T. Higgins

Jonathan Higgins

Scale 20,000
0 10 20 40 60 80 100 150.

ROCK HARBOR

Salt Works
Mrs L. Crosby
E. Cole
B. Walker
J. Sherman

Salt Works
J. Nickerson
P. S. Harding

EASTHAM
Creek
T. Smith

ORLEANS

A. Freeman
S. Smith
H. Doane
D. Smith
R. Nickerson
H. Harding
L. Hurd

J. L. Crosby's
Shoe Store
J. Hopkins Jr
J. Martin
T. Nickerson

E. Higgins

F. Young
Jarvis
J. A. Rogers Store
J. G. Sloan
S. Rogers
L. Northrop
W. E. Smith
E. Hurd
J. Horton
D. Smith
S. K. Smith

Rogers
Rogers
Stevens
Mrs T Crosby
Mrs L Snow
J. Snow
Mrs D Snow
F. Sherman
J. Smith

P. Rogers

O. Crosby
L. Rogers

J. Cummings
B. Hurd
D. G. Smith
S. H. Smith
S. N. Smith
L. Young

Scale 20,000
0 10 20 40 60 80 100

Billingsgate Shoal

N. E. by E.

E. N. E.

E. by N. 3/4 N

77

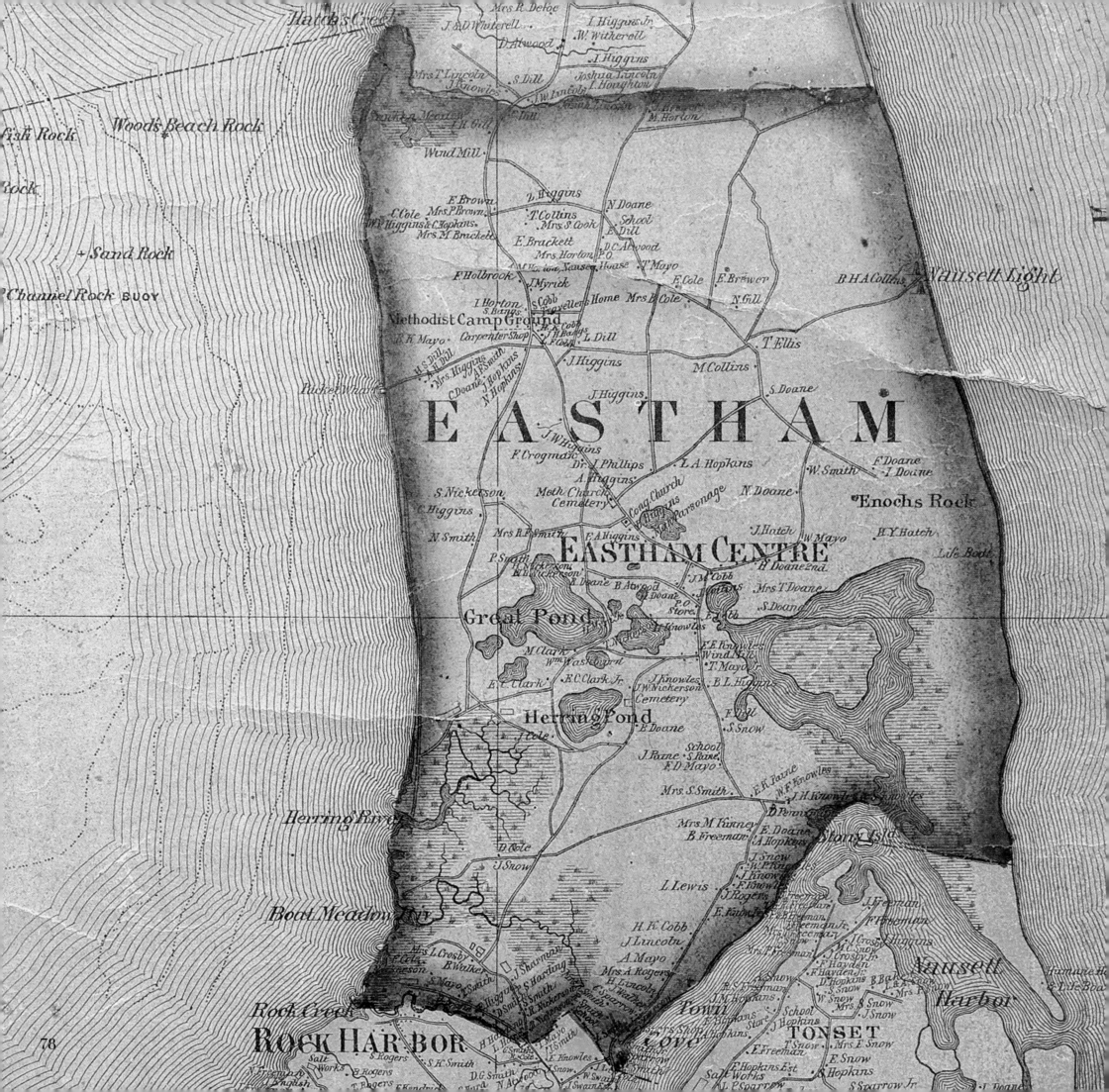

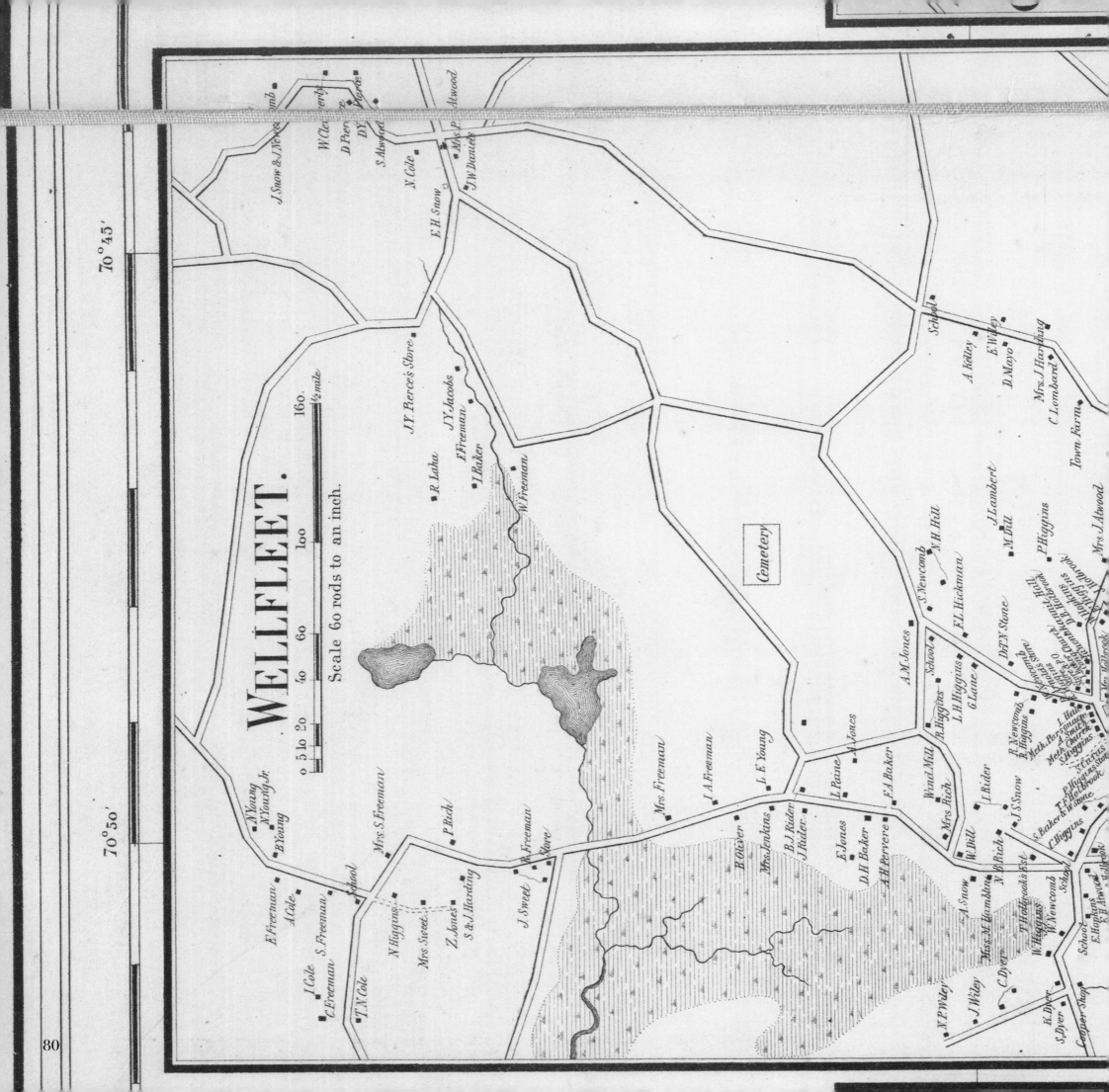

WELLFLEET.

0 5 10 20 40 60 100 160.

Scale 60 rods to an inch.

½ mile

70° 45'

70° 50'

Cemetery

School

Town Farm

School

J. Snow & J. Newcomb
W. Clenderby
D. Pierce
D.Y.
S. Atwood
Mrs. P. Atwood
N. Cole
E. H. Snow
J. W. Daniels

J.Y. Perce's Store
J.N. Jacobs
R. Laha
F. Freeman
I. Baker
W. Freeman

N. Young
N. Young Jr.
B. Young
Mrs. S. Freeman
P. Rich
R. Freeman
Store

F. Freeman
A. Cole
I. Cole
C. Freeman
S. Freeman
T. N. Cole
School
N. Higgins
Mrs. Sweet
Z. Jones
S. & J. Harding
J. Sweet

Mrs. Freeman
I. A. Freeman
J. E. Young
A. M. Jones
M. Jones
L. Paine
F. J. Baker
Wind Mill
Mrs. Rich
B. Oliver
Mrs. Jenkins
B. J. Rider
J. Rider
E. Jones
D. H. Baker
A. H. Pervere

S. Newcomb
N. H. Hill
F. L. Hickman
R. Higgins
L. H. Higgins
G. Lane
Dr.T.N. Stone
School
J. Lambert
M. Dill
P. Higgins
A. Kelley
E. Wiley
D. Mayo
Mrs. J. Harding
C. Lombard

R. Newcomb
R. Higgins
Meth. Parsonage
Meth. Church
S. Higgins
J. Rider
J. S. Snow
W. Dill
N. Rich
C. Higgins

N. P. Wiley
J. Wiley
C. Dyer
Miss M. Hamblin
P. Higgins
T. Higgins St.
W. Higgins
W. Newcomb
School
A. Snow
E. Hopkins
J. Smith
T. F. Holbrook

K. Dyer
S. Dyer
Cooper Shop

80

WELLFLEET HARBOR

Light House

Commercial Wharf

Store Houses

Enterprise Wharf

Store Houses

Store S.Higgins

Store Houses

B.H.Freeman
& J.B.Harding

J.C.Rich

J.Sparrow

E.Higgins

Mrs.W.Stubbs

S.R.Hawes

J.Chipman
Shoe Shop

O.Boone

E.Higgins

J.Freeman

E.Collins
Shop

E.Collins

Store

W.M.Baker

W.H.Wiley's Fork & Shop

W.Kemp

J.Freeman

J.Holbrook

A.H.Kemp

D.Newcomb

T.Hawes

I.B.Hawes

S.Kemp Jr.

J.Graham

S.Holbrook

W.Kemp

W.Jordan

A.C.Harding

Mrs.H.Lewis

D.Atwood

D.Abwood

J.H.Atwood

S.M.Coval

B.Wiley

D.Chipman

E.Chipman

W.Nickerson

C.Gorham

S.Higgins

E.Gorham

S.Young

School

S.C.Chipman

S.M. anmae

J. Higgins

H.Atwood

E.Wiley

Salt
Works

BARNSTABLE VILLAGE

J.Marchant
Nelson

D.Loring

D.Eldridge

Grist Mill

P.Maristppa

C.Stetson

N.Crocker

A.H.Young

F.&I.Lewis

W.Hinckley 2nd

W.I.Lewis

E.Loring

W.Hinckley

Allinckley

B.Crocker

R.Stephens

Harris

Store

Mrs.M.Nickerson

L.Davis

J.Chamberlain

S.S.Crocker

W.D.Lewis

Parsonage

Jenkins Tin Shop & Store

J.Andrews

I.Chipman

W.Chipman

J.Baker

Bapt.Church

Hedy Davis

T.Holmes

T.Holmes

J.Parker

J.Davis

J.Wilson

W.Chapman

Tin Shop

C.S.Shop

K.R.Smith

Dr.W.Allen

Mrs.N.Davis

J.Hall

Mrs.D.Crowell

Mrs.A.Clark

J.Hinckley

E.Hinckley

J.Hinckley

E.Smith

Mrs.B.Hinckley

Mrs.J.Lowe &

Crocker

Mrs.J.Hinckley Jr.

Mrs.A.Amable

F.Crocker

Lewis

B.Davis

SOUTH TRURO

Round Pond

Higgins Pond

Newcomb's Pond

Herring Pond

Round Brook Island

TRURO VILLAGE

Scale 20,000

Cemetery
Meth. Church

Wind Mill
Cong. Church

Town Hall

Meth. Parsonage

Town Farm

School

Store

North Branch

Mill Pond

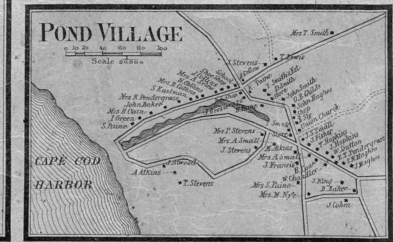

PROVINCETOWN VILLAGE

Scale 1/8000

Cemetery

BUSINESS DIRECTORY

BANKS.
Provincetown Bank, N. Freeman Prest. Elisha Smith Cashr. Commercial St.
Seamans Savings Bank, R.E. Nickerson Treasr. Union Exchange

INSURANCE OFFICES.
Atlantic Mutual Insurance Co. R.E. Nickerson Secry. Union Exch.
Equitable Marine — N.D. Freeman Secry. Commercial St.

SHIP STORES.
Union Wharf Co. — Commercial Street
E.S. Smith & Co. — Central Wharf
J.E. & G. Bowley — Bowley's Wharf
Paine Nickerson & Co. — Union Exchange
T. & J.H. Hilliard & Co. — Commercial Wharf
Freeman & Chapman — Commercial Street
Paine & Emery
Daniel Small
E. & E.K. Cook
S. Cook Jun.
D. Conwell
Nickerson & Tuck — City Wharf
H. & S. Cook & Co. — Eastern Packet Pier

DRY GOODS DEALERS.
Charles Nickerson — Commercial Street
Rufus Conant Jun.
Caleb Nickerson & Son
S.A. Paine
Godfrey Rider Jun.
J. & N. Lewis

GROCERY & PROVISION DEAs.
Phillip Cook — Commercial Street
Jesse Small
R. Soper
F.M. Freeman
Carson & Co
Benj. Lancy Jun.
J. & N. Lewis
D.C. Cobb
John Smith
S.D. Cook, Central Market
Caleb Cook, Row Market
E. Nickerson
D.S. Small
Henry Dyer
S.M. Smith, Flour & Grain Store

CLOTHING DEALERS.
J.F. Small — Commercial Street
W. Boyne

MILLINERY & FANCY GOODS.
Godfrey Rider Jun. — Commercial Street
Ann Nickerson
Mrs. S.A. Paine

VARIETY STORES.
H. Willard — Commercial Street

FURNITURE DEALERS.
Baker & Seller, Cook's Block Commercial Street

JEWELLERS.
Dudley & Long — Commercial Street

DENTISTS.
Dr. A.S. Dudley — Commercial Street

SAIL MAKERS.
C.A. Hannum — Union Wharf
F.A. Paine — Central Wharf
Paul Atkins — Commercial Street
C.D. Cook
S. Bangs Jun. Bangs Whf.
C.H. Dyer
Baxter & Pettis — Market Wharf
J. Hall — Commercial Wharf

SHIP SMITHS.
Ward & Alexander — Union Wharf
I.A. Small — Central
R.C. Hartford — Market

PAINTERS & GLAZIERS.
John Williams — Central Wharf
G.F. Twombly & Co. — Commercial Street
Alfred Nickerson — Union Wharf

BOAT BUILDERS.
W.W. Smith — Commercial Street
D.S. Kelley
O. Snow — Wharf

SHIP CARPRS. & SPAR MAKERS
E.G. Loring — Central Wharf
Nathl. Hopkins — Union Wharf
B. Knowles Carpenter &c. Commercial Street
L.L. Smith

MASON
A. Hamlen — Commercial Street

LUMBER DEALER.
E.W. Holway, Planning Mill. Commercial Street

STOVES & TIN WARE DEARS
J. Engles — Central Wharf
C.B. Snow — Commercial Street

BOOTS & SHOES.
L. Young — Commercial Street

PHYSICIANS.
Dr. J. Stone — Commercial Street
Dr. S.A. Paine
Dr. John L. Lothrop

HOTELS.
Pilgrim House James Gifford Propr. Commercial St.
Union House — Commercial Street

SALOONS.
Ocean Saloon W. Allerton — Commercial Street

COOPER.
Geo. DeWolf, Oil & Water Cask Mfr. Freemans Wharf

BROKER.
R.E. Nickerson — Union Exchange

PRINTERS.
J.W. Emery Provincetown Banner. Commercial Street

DEPTY COLLECTOR
S.S. Gifford — Commercial Street
Elisha Dyer, Town Clerk
R. Stevens Supt. Marine Railway, Union Wharf.

MASTERS OF VESSELS
Capt. J. Kilburn — Capt. J. Swift
Young — H. Sparks
S.S. Young — T.A. Miller
L. Mayo — T. Lewis
A. Smith — D. Conway
Rufus Hopkins — E. Tillson.

POND VILLAGE
Scale 1/8000

CAPE COD HARBOR

84

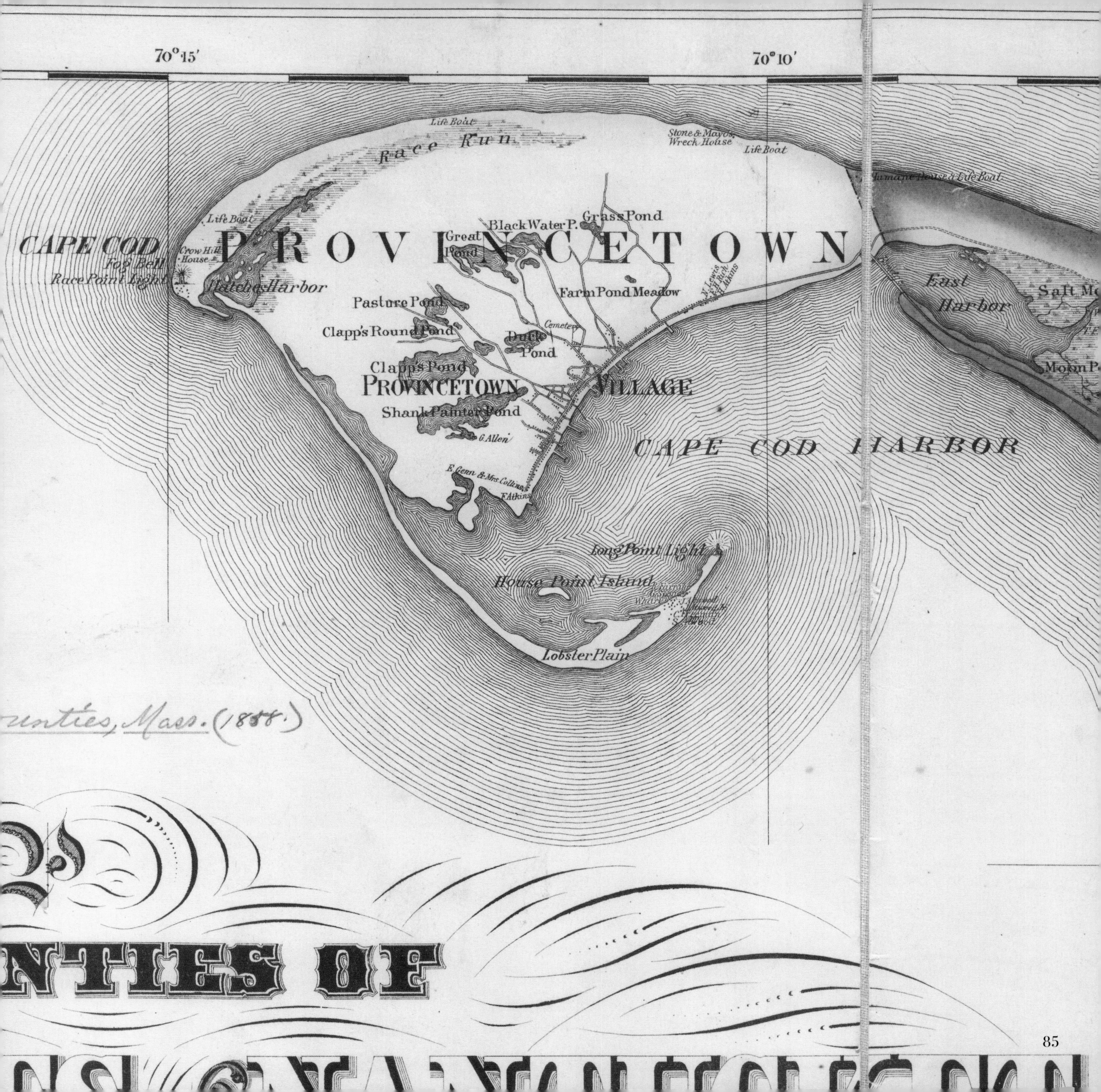

Life Boat

Race Run

Stone & Mayos,
Wreck House

Life Boat

Humane House & Life Boat

Life Boat

CAPE COD

P R O V I N C E T O W N

Black Water P.

Grass Pond

Great
Pond

Crow Hill
House

Fog Bell

Race Point Light

Hatches Harbor

East
Harbor

Salt M

Farm Pond Meadow

N. Lewis
W. Rich
G.F. Adams

Pasture Pond

Cemetery

Clapp's Round Pond

Duck
Pond

Clapps Pond

PROVINCETOWN

VILLAGE

Moon P

Shank Painter Pond

CAPE COD HARBOR

G. Allen

E. Genn & Mrs. Collins

F Atkin

Long Point Light

House Point Island

unties, Mass. (1858.)

Lobster Plain

NTIES OF

85

PROVINCETOWN

0 5 1o 2o   4o   6o

Scale $\frac{1}{8000}$.

Mrs. Phillbrook

R. Hill
A. Pierce
J. Smith

Cemetery

J. Kilburn

W. Whelding
N. Whelding   G. Ryder   J. Worms   Salt Works   J. Baker
W. Mathews   H. Holmes
N. White   A. Garland   Knowles
                  A. Adams   N. W. Conant   J. Cook
                                                        Fitch   D. Sparks
                                                        T. Garrett
                                                        D. S. Small
C. Burkit   T. P. Johnson
T. Johnson   E. Ryder R. Ryder
Mrs. Parker   S. Nickerson   N. Ryder S. Ryder
Town Asylum   Sprague   W. Pierce   R. Knowles
Williams   Pilgrim Hos.
Mrs. Paine   S. Sofford
H. Harvender   N. Freeman
J. H. Harvender   T. Hilliard
                     R. Hillary   K. W. Freeman
                     School   J. Young   N. Holmes
Town Hall   Meth. Parsonage   Mrs. Atkins
                     Mrs. Atkins   S. Smith
                     Rev. O. Myrick   O. Wyer
                     G. Ridder   J. Crocker
Meth. Church   Dr. Whitney   S. Nickerson   Small
                     J. M. Cook   J. Atkins
G. H. Cornell   J. Eldridge
E. C. Brien
Dr. A. S. Dudley
S. M. Smith
R. Paine   P. O.
D. Fairbanks
T. Lathrop   J. Nickerson
A. Crocker   D. Crocker
R. Crocker

J. Foster   J. M. Nickerson   Atwood   J. Williams Town House   Rider's Wharf
Cemetery   Z. Higgins   G. De Wolf   B. L. Cook
                   S. P. Snow   J. Nickerson
S. D. Cook   R. Young   T. Fenn
                   Nickerson   L. Cook
A. Gill   O. Smith   N. Young
                                       N. Snow

86

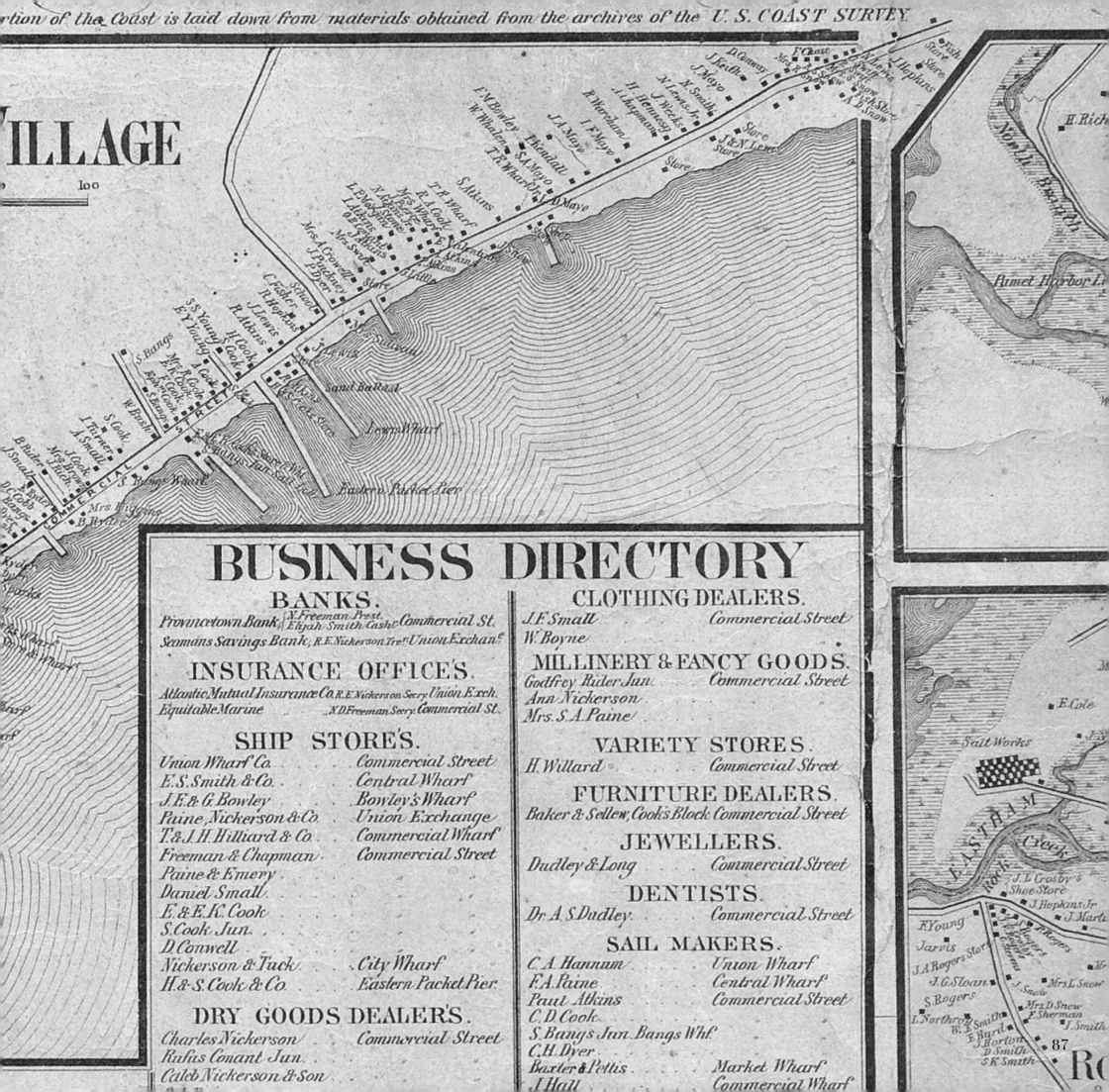

VILLAGE

100

BUSINESS DIRECTORY

BANKS.

Provincetown Bank | N. Freeman Prest. Elijah Smith Cashr. Commercial St.
Seamans Savings Bank, R.E. Nickerson Trer. Union Exchange

INSURANCE OFFICES.

Atlantic Mutual Insurance Co. R.E. Nickerson Secry. Union Exch.
Equitable Marine | N.D. Freeman Secry. Commercial St.

SHIP STORES.

Union Wharf Co. . . . . Commercial Street
E.S. Smith & Co. . . . . Central Wharf
J.E. & G. Bowley . . . . Bowley's Wharf
Paine, Nickerson & Co. . . Union Exchange
T. & J.H. Hilliard & Co. . . Commercial Wharf
Freeman & Chapman . . . Commercial Street
Paine & Emery .
Daniel Small .
E. & E.K. Cook .
S. Cook Jun.
D. Conwell .
Nickerson & Tuck . . . . City Wharf
H. & S. Cook & Co. . . . . Eastern Packet Pier.

DRY GOODS DEALERS.

Charles Nickerson . . . . Commercial Street
Rufus Conant Jun.
Caleb Nickerson & Son

CLOTHING DEALERS.

J.F. Small . . . . . . Commercial Street
W. Boyne

MILLINERY & FANCY GOODS.

Godfrey Rider Jun. . . . . Commercial Street
Ann Nickerson .
Mrs. S.A. Paine .

VARIETY STORES.

H. Willard . . . . . . Commercial Street

FURNITURE DEALERS.

Baker & Sellew, Cook's Block Commercial Street

JEWELLERS.

Dudley & Long . . . . . . Commercial Street

DENTISTS.

Dr. A.S. Dudley . . . . . . Commercial Street

SAIL MAKERS.

C.A. Hannum . . . . . Union Wharf
F.A. Paine . . . . . Central Wharf
Paul Atkins . . . . . Commercial Street
C.D. Cook .
S. Bangs Jun. Bangs Whf.
C.H. Dyer .
Baxter & Pettis . . . . . Market Wharf
J. Hall . . . . . . Commercial Wharf

87

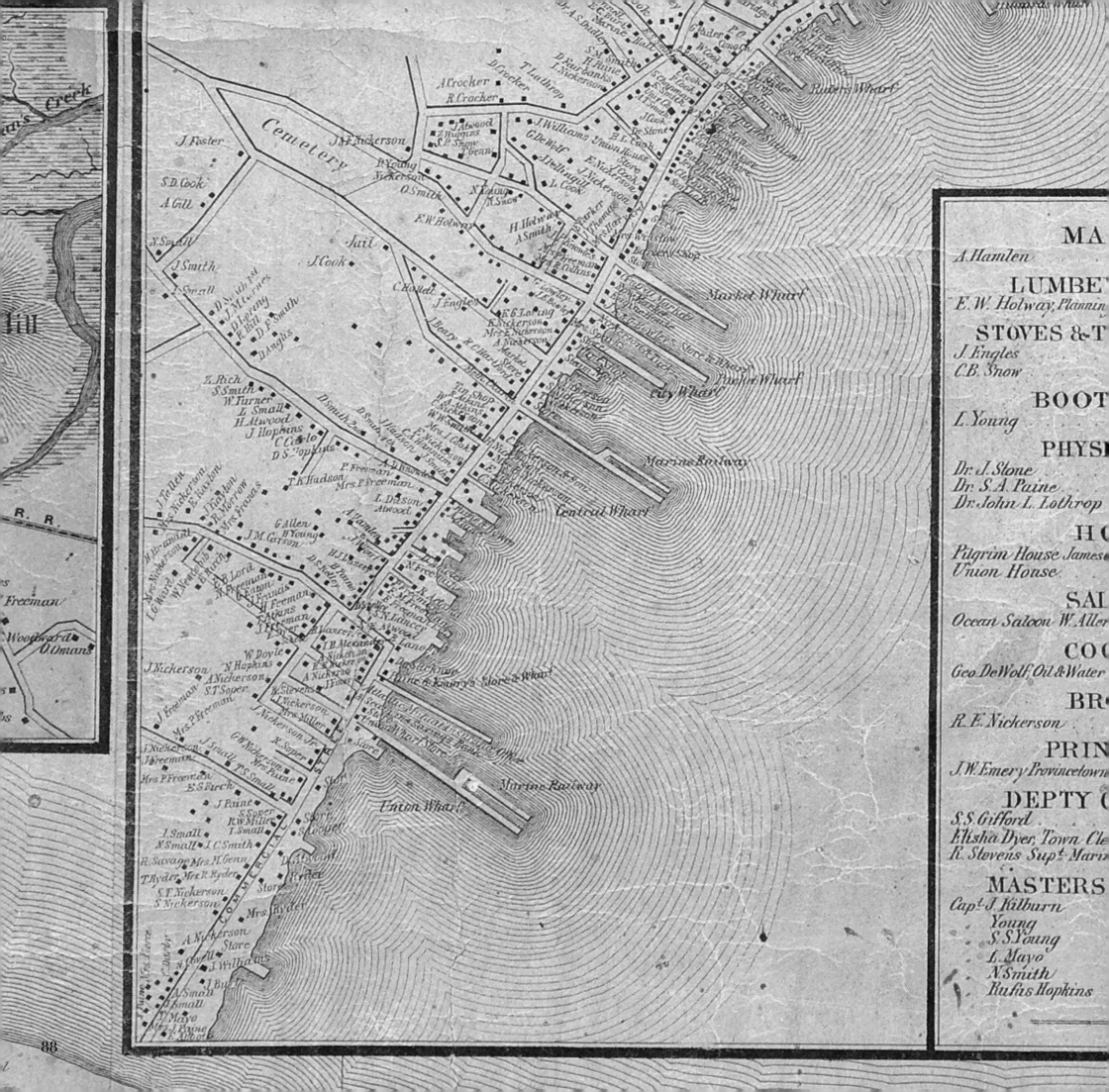

Daniel Small

E. & E.K. Cook

S. Cook Jun.

D. Conwell

Nickerson & Tuck . . . . . City Wharf

H. & S. Cook & Co. . . . . Eastern Packet Pier.

DRY GOODS DEALER'S.

Charles Nickerson . . . . Commercial Street

Rufus Conant Jun.

Caleb Nickerson & Son

S.A. Paine

Godfrey Rider Jun.

J. & N. Lewis

GROCERY & PROVISION DEAS

Phillip Cook . . . . . . Commercial Street

Jesse Small

R. Soper

F.M. Freeman

Carson & Co

Benj. Lancy Jun.

J. & N. Lewis

D.C. Cobb.

John Smith

S.D. Cook, Central Market

Caleb Cook, Row Market

E. Nickerson

D.S. Small.

Henry Dyer

S.M. Smith, Flour & Grain Store

DENTISTS.

Dr. A.S. Dudley . . . . . Commercial Street

SAIL MAKERS.

C.A. Hannum . . . . . . Union Wharf

F.A. Paine . . . . Central Wharf

Paul Atkins . . . . . . Commercial Street

C.D. Cook

S. Bangs Jun. Bangs Whf.

C.H. Dyer.

Baxter & Pettis . . . . . Market Wharf

J. Hall . . . . Commercial Wharf

SHIP SMITHS.

Ward & Alexander . . . . Union Wharf

I.A. Small . . . . Central

R.C. Hartford . . . . . . Market

PAINTERS & GLAZIERS.

John Williams . . . . . Central Wharf

G.F. Twombly & Co. . . . Commercial Street

Alfred Nickerson . . . . Union Wharf

BOAT BUILDERS.

W.W. Smith . . . . . . Commercial Street

D.S. Kelley

O. Snow. . . . . Wharf

SHIP CARPRS & SPAR MAKERS

E.G. Loring . . . . . . Central Wharf

Nathl. Hopkins . . . . . Union Wharf

R. Knowles Carpenter &c. Commercial Street

L.L. Smith

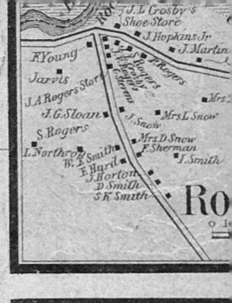

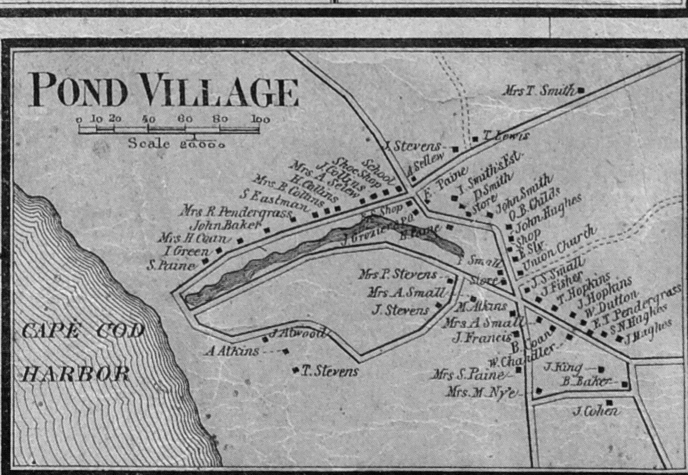

POND VILLAGE

Scale 20.000

CAPE COD HARBOR

89

SQUIBNOCKET

Beach

Alma Mayhew   J. Mayhew

BUSINESS DIRECTORY,
FOR HOLMES HOLE.
MERCHANT TRADERS &c.

Thos Bradley & Sons, Dry Goods & Groceries Main St
Thos Robinson, ... " "
W. Crocker & Co. . . . . . . " "
Thos Barrows, ... " "
E. W. Coffin, ... " "
J. M. Taber, ... " "
W. C. Luce, ... Union Whf
Holmes & Brothers, ... Neck
J. S. Luce , Stoves & Tin Ware . . . Union Wh
Nye & Jenkins, Paint Store . . . Main St
M. P. Butler, Market . . . . Union Whf
J. W. Howland, Lumber Dealer . . .
J. F. Robinson, Carpenter . . . .
J. T. James, ... Main St.
T. Luce, Boots & Shoes . . . .
Presbry Norton, Boat Builder . . . " "
D. A. Cleveland, Physician . . . " "
H. P. Worth, Depty Collector . . . " "

BUSINESS DIRECTORY.
FOR EDGARTOWN.

Marthas Vineyard Bank, Corner Main & Water St.
Dr. D Fisher Prest. J. T Pease Cashr

CUSTOM HOUSE OFFICRs.

Constant Norton, Collector
E. P. Coffin, Depty

PHYSICIANS

Dr. J. Pierse, ... Office Main St.
W. T. S. Brackett, ... " "
E. Maybury . . . . . " "
I. H. Lucas . . . . . Water St.

ATTORNEY AT LAW.

David Davis . . . . . . Main St.

DRY GOODS & CLOTHING DEALrs

J. N. Vinson, Dry Goods . . . A Main St.
J. W. Coffin
S. Osborn Jr. Clothing & Dry Goods . .
I. Norton . . . . . . "
S. L. Pease, P. O. & Store . . . "

MERCHANT TAILOR

J. H Munroe . . . . Corner Main & Water St

GROCERY & PROVISION DEAs.

J. Dillingham, ...
R. Cleveland, ... Main St.
E. G Pease, ... " "
C. B. Marchant . . . . . " "
Wm Bradley, Grocer & Hardware . . " "
Holly & Fisher, Grain & Flour . . .
E. C. Cornell, Confectionary & Perfumery
Fish & Smith Painters . . . Water street
J. M. Mayhew, Sail Maker . . Mayhew Whf
E. R. Dunham, House Carpenter . . Water St
C. F. Dunham, Ship Smith . . .
T. E. Butler, Cooper . . . . "
H. Ripley, Lumber Dealer . . . "

HOTELS

Edgartown Hotel J. R. Norton Propr. Water St.
Marcy House L. Marcy
J. Mayhew, Express

Colors Ex

19 Tertiar
20 Drift
21 Alluviu

New

Cutty

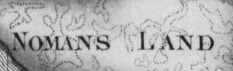

NOMANS LAND

70°50'   70°45'

Dukes County

EAST FALMOUTH
Scale 50.000

HOLMES' HOLE
Scale 8.000

WEST TISBURY
Scale 20.000

EDGARTOWN
Scale 8.000

ELIZABETH ISL'

NAUSH'

PASQUE

NASHAWENA

Quicks Hole

Robinsons Hole

Kettle Cove

Tarpaulin Cove

French Watering Place

DUKE'S VINEYARD S

Cedar Tree Nock

Cape Higgon

Menamsha Bight

Gay Head Cliffs

Gay Head Light

GAY HEAD

Indian Lands

Menamsha Pond

Nashaquitsa Pond

Squibnocket Pond

Squibnocket Beach

SQUIBNOCKET

NASHAQUITSA

CHRISTIANTOWN

Indian Hill

James Pond

Lumbards Cove

Pauls Point

MIDDLE TOWN

TISBURY

MARTHA'S

WEST TISBURY VILLAGE

Prospect Hill

CHILMARK

Peaked Hill

QUANSUE
Great Tisbury P

Chilmark Pond

Black Point Pond

Tyers Cove

Deep

Muddy Cove

Tashmoo Pond

CAPE COD

GEOLOGICAL MAP
OF
BARNSTABLE, DUKES & NANTUCKET COUNTIES
MASSACHUSETTS.
By Edward Hitchcock.

Scale 10 Miles to an inch.

Colors Explained.

BUSINESS DIRECTORY

Mishaum Point

B U

41°30'

WEST FALMOUTH

B.Crowell
R.Landers   S.G.Cahoon
A.Bowman
J.Gifford
A.Crowell   E.Landers
Bowman
Mrs.Hatch
Mrs.Bradley Es.   S.A.Gifford
E.Bowman   School
J.Bowman   J.Small
                  L.Bowman
S.Bowman
N.Eldred
S.Swift
Wind Mill   Meth.Church
G.H.Baker
J.Gifford   Union Store & P.O.
Wharf W.Baker
                  Lucy Eldred
S.Swift   J.Bowman
                  C.Bowman
                  D.Bowman
                  J.Swift
Friends Meeting House
D.Swift   Store
S.Swift
Paint
Mill L.M.Wing   B.S.Swift
S.Dillingham
J.Boyce   J.Baxter
W.Dillingham
                  A.Dillingham
                  N.Coleman
                  S.Allen
Z.Fisk
S.Gifford   School
Pt.Bowerman
B.Baker   A.Swift
M.F.Weeks
L.C.Fish   G.W.Weeks
Mrs.Weeks
A.S.Tobr   L.Landers
A.S.Gifford
                  B.Swift
Scale 1/30,000   1/2 mile
0 10 20 30   80   160 rods

Salt Works

EAST FALMOUTH

A.Crocker
H.Eldredge
Factory Co.
Woolen Mill
Mrs.Crocker
                  J.Robinson's Sons
                  A.Green
                  A.Baxter
                  Foster Store & P.O.
                  School
Paint Shop   D.Swift
T.Lewis   W.Jenkins
J.Tobey   S.Crowell
T.Lewis
J.Tobey Grist Mill
         A.Baxter
Scale 1/30,000   1/2 mile
0 10 20 30   80   160 rods

E L I Z A B E T H   I S L

Pennikese or Pine Island

Gull Island

PASQUE

Robinsons Hole

Quicks Hole

U   K

D   N A S H A W E N A

Copicut   Pease Ledge
Cuttyhunk Pond
Canapitsett

CUTTYHUNK

41°25'

Cuttyhunk Light

Gosnold's Pond

Saw and Hog Reef
Rocky
Saw Rock

HOLMES'HOLE
Scale 1/8,000
0 5 10 20   40   60 rods

T.Luce Es.
B.Weeks   Mrs.Dunham
Mrs.Couch
A.Luce   Mrs.L.Smith
                  G.Smith
T.Luce   J.Robinson
L.Luce   T.Smith
C.Tilton   J.Smith
J.F.Robinson   J.Mayo
L.Daggett   J.Dias
                  Shop
B.Herschell   Betsey Baker
                  L.Smith
Mrs.Daggett   Mrs.Manter
H.Manter   Mrs.R.Crowell
T.Downer   R.Lambert
T.Bradley   B.Luce
                  J.Crocker

Town House
Mrs.Hancock
S.Thompson

T.Cathcart

Cemetery
Cong.Church

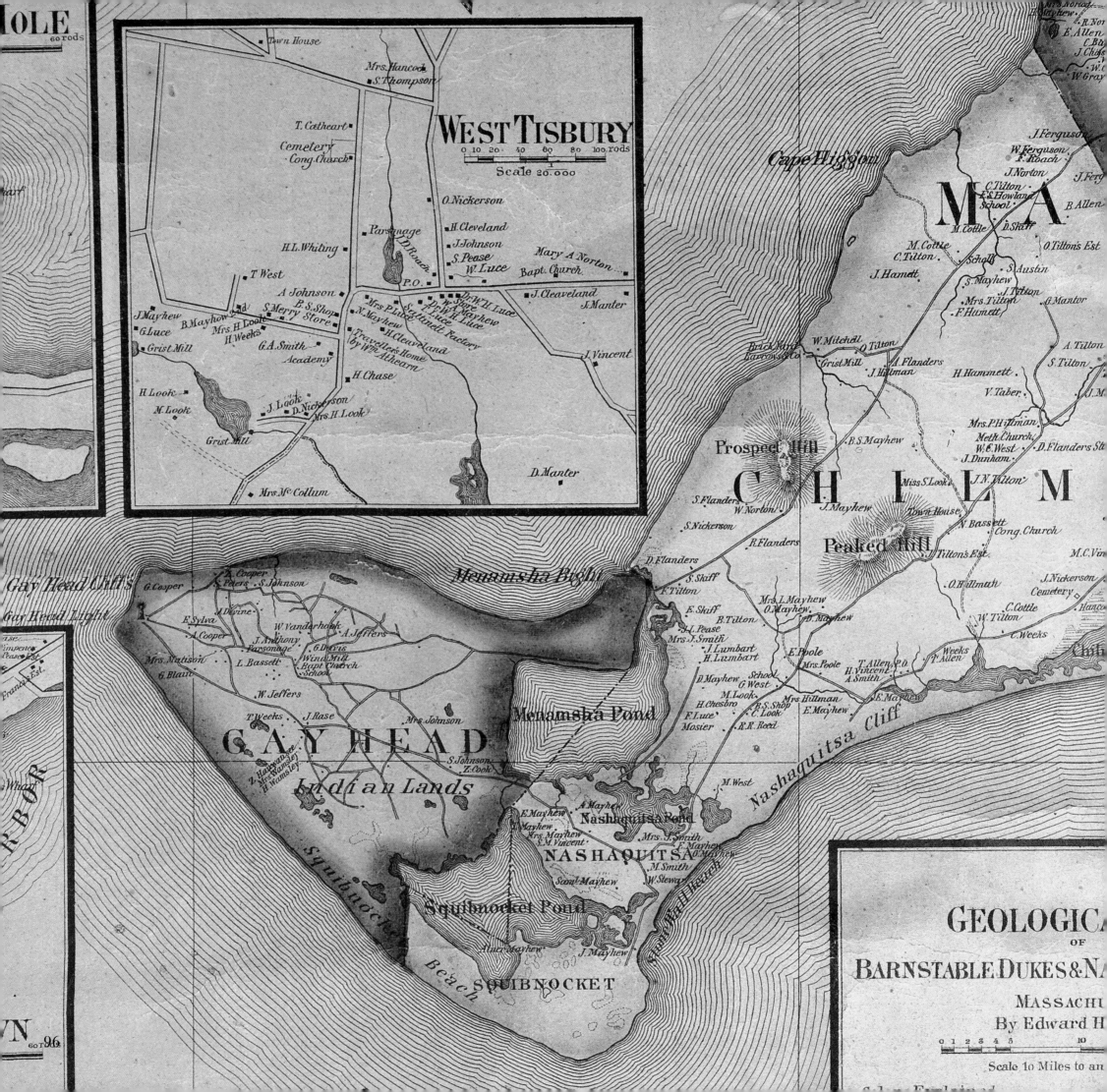

OLE
60 rods

WEST TISBURY
0 10 20   40   60   80 100 rods
Scale 20.000

Town House

Mrs. Hancock
S. Thompson

T. Cathcart
Cemetery
Cong. Church

O. Nickerson

H. Cleveland
J. Johnson
S. Pease
W. Luce
Mary A. Norton
Bapt. Church

Parsonage
D. Roach
H. L. Whiting
P.O.

T. West
A. Johnson
B. S. Shop
S. Merry Store
Dr. W. H. Luce
Dr. W. A. Mayhew
Luce Luce
Dr. W. H. Luce
J. Cleaveland
J. Manter

J. Mayhew
B. Mayhew
Mrs. H. Look
H. Weeks
Mrs. P. Look
N. Mayhew
Scattinett Factory

G. Luce
Grist Mill
G. A. Smith
H. Cleaveland
Traveller's Home
by Wm. Athearn
J. Vincent

Academy

H. Chase

H. Look
M. Look
J. Look
D. Nickerson
Mrs. H. Look

Grist Mill

Mrs. McCollum
D. Manter

Cape Higgon

J. Ferguson
W. Ferguson
F. Roach
J. Norton
C. Tilton
F. S. Howland
School

M A

M. Cottle
D. Skiff
B. Allen
O. Tilton's Est
M. Cottle
C. Tilton
School
S. Austin
J. Hamett
S. Mayhew
J. Tilton
Mrs. Tilton
O. Mantor
F. Humett

Brick Yard
Barrows & Co
W. Mitchell
O. Tilton
Grist Mill
A. Flanders
J. Hillman
H. Hammett
A. Tilton
S. Tilton
V. Taber
J. M.

CH   IL   M

Prospect Hill
B. S. Mayhew
Mrs. P. Hillman
Meth. Church
W. C. West
J. Dunham
D. Flanders Sti

S. Flanders
W. Norton
J. Mayhew
Town House
Miss S. Look
J. N. Tilton
N. Bassett
Cong. Church

S. Nickerson
Peaked Hill
Tilton's Est
M. C. Vin

R. Flanders
O. Hillman
J. Nickerson
Cemetery

D. Flanders
S. Skiff
Mrs. L. Mayhew
O. Mayhew
D. Mayhew
C. Cottle
Hanco

F. Tilton
E. Skiff
B. Tilton
W. Tilton

Menamsha Bight
H. L. Pease
Mrs. J. Smith
C. Weeks

Gay Head Cliffs
G. Cooper
Z. Cooper
Peters
S. Johnson

J. Lumbart
H. Lumbart
E. Poole
T. Allen
P.O.
Weeks
T. Allen

Gay Head Light
E. Sylva
W. Vanderhoop
A. Jeffers
Mrs. Poole
H. Vincent
A. Smith

A. Cooper
J. Devine
G. Davis
D. Mayhew
School
G. West
E. Mayhew

se
impence
Pease Est
Mrs. Matison
J. Anthony
Parsonage
Wind Mill
Bapt. Church
School
M. Look
H. Chesbro
Mrs. Hillman
E. Mayhew
E. Ma

Frank St

L. Bassett
G. Blain
F. Luce
Mosier
C. Look
R. R. Reed
B. S. Shop

W. Jeffers

GAY HEAD
Menamsha Pond

R B O R

T. Weeks
J. Rase
Mrs. Johnson
M. West
Nashaquitsa Cliff

Wharf
Z. Harrison
Mrs. Womsley
H. Womsley
S. Johnson
Z. Cook
Indian Lands

A. Mayhew
E. Mayhew
Mayhew
Mrs. J. Smith
Nashaquitsa Pond
Mrs. S. M. Vincent
E. Mayhew
O. Mayhew

NASHAQUITSA
M. Smith
W. Stewart

Saml. Mayhew

Squibnocket Pond
J. Mayhew

Beach
SQUIBNOCKET

GEOLOGICA
OF
BARNSTABLE DUKES & NA
MASSACHU
By Edward H

0 1 2 3 4 5   10
Scale 10 Miles to an

N
60 rods
96

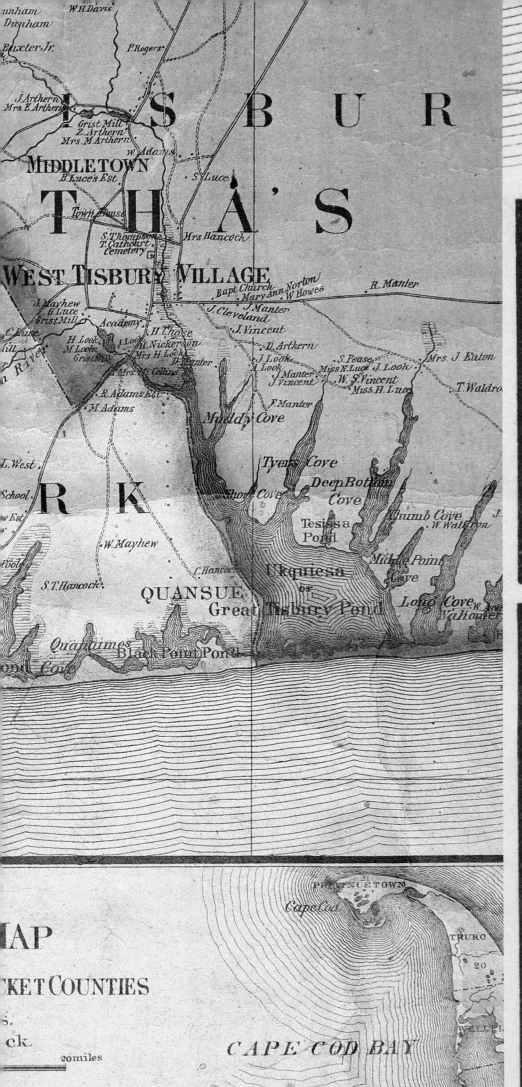

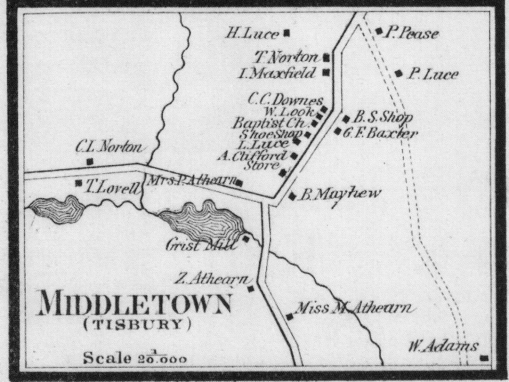

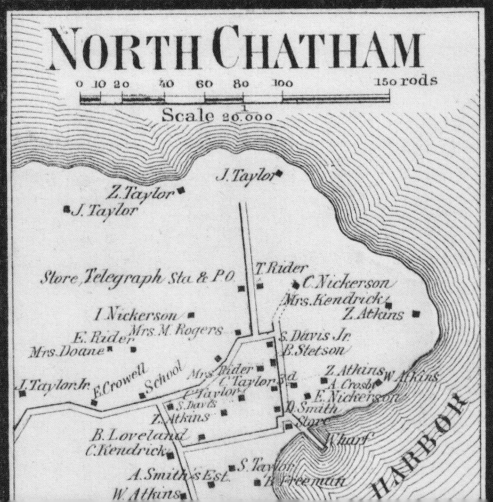

97

HOLMES' HOLE

Scale $\frac{1}{8.000}$

0 5 10 20 40 60 rods

Cuttyhunk Pond

TYHUNK

Canapitsett

T. Luce Est.
W. Weekes
Mrs Couch
Mrs Dunham
A. Crowell
Mrs L Smith
G. Smith
T. Luce
L. Luce
T. Robinson
C. West
J. Merry
T. Smith
C. Tilton
J. Smith
J. Crowell
J. F. Robinson's
J. Dius
L. Daggett
Shop
R. Herschelt
Betsey Butler
L. Smith
Mrs Manter
Mrs Daggett
J. Gray
Mrs M Crowell
H. Manter
Shoe Shop
F. Lambert
C. Downey
R. Dexter
W. C. Luce
W. Dowens
T. Bradley
C. Downey's
Paint Shop
Mrs A. Manchester
T. H. Smith
J. Luce
W. Crocker
R. W. Crocker
W. Norton
G. Harding
J. S. Adams
A. Daggett
Meth Church P.O.
Store
C. Smith
Tin Shop
Carriage Shop
B. Downes
Capack Hall
Shop
Luce
Store
Cooper Shop
P. Norton
F. Daggett
J. West
Mrs Luce
G. Dunham
Store House
B. Shop
Mrs C. Dexter
School
H. Robinson
C. G. Smith
Union Wharf
W. Luce
N. S. Smith
T. Barrow
Mrs Bliss
P. Norton
Mrs Dexter
T. Barrow
E. Dillingham
B. Clough
H. Nye
J. Cottle
Store
Dr R. F. Jones
Dr F. Worth
T. Barrow
Observatory
J. M. Taber
P. Barrows
W. Harding
W. Merry
W. West
T. Harding
Custom H.
P. Luce
C. Smith
E. Harding
Bapt. Ch.
G. Smith
T. Hillman
B. C. Cromwell
E. Dexter
Worth
A. H. Anthony
C. P. Barrows
B. Merry
Store
Bradley
J. W. Howlands
Mrs Dillingham
Cong. Church
T. Bradley's Store
Carpenters Shop
Weeks
Lumber Yard
H. Chase
Mrs Robinson
C. Smith
S. Daggett & J. Bradley
A. Newcomb
Shop
Mansion House
Mrs Branscomb
G. G. Look
H. Beetle
T. Bradley
Store
Mrs Evans comb
B. Nye
Livery Stable
J. A. Swain
Shoe Shop
G. Luce
T. Hillman
T. Tuckerman
T. Robinson
J. West
J. Gibbins
T. Tilton
R. G. Luce
Store
G. Luce
C. Harding
W. Lambert
B. Allen
G. Daggett
M. P. Butler
J. Crowell
A. Luce
P. Linch
School
E. Smith
T. Hillman
Maria A Yale
T. Hillman
J. D. Peaks
W. Buckley
Shop
F. Brown
Mrs C. Luce
T. Bradley
T. Foster
Mrs Buckley
H. Dexter
Mrs S. Dexter
Miss M. Norton
Meth. Parsonage
Mrs Hannah Lambert
W. Cleaveland
J. T. James
B. Reynolds
P. Cromwell
P. Barrows
M. Norton
J. Cleaveland
Cemetery

Dr J. Pierse
D. Smith
S. Huxford
E. Buller
E. Luce
J. Mayhew
M. Evernac
H. Norton
99

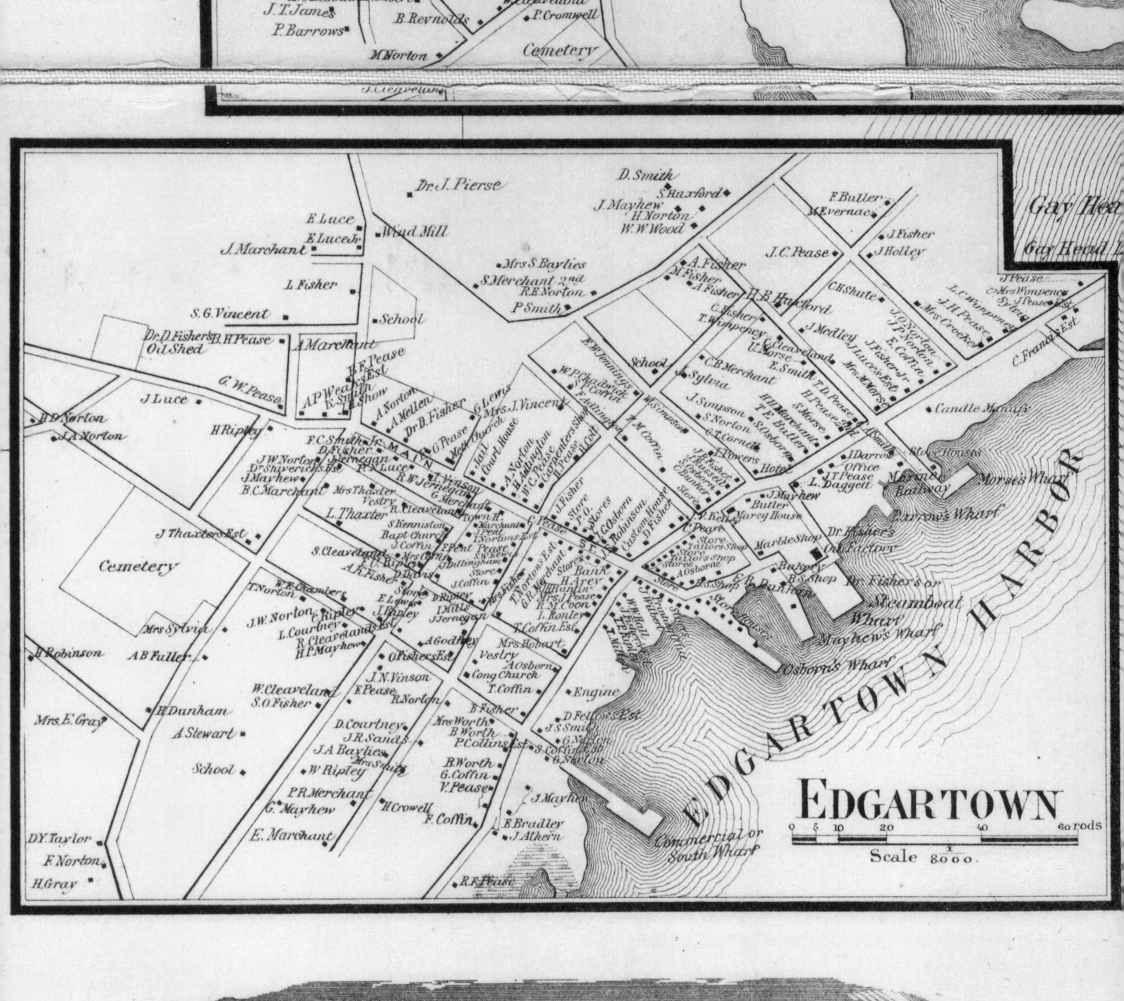

EDGARTOWN

Gay Hea
Gay Head

EDGARTOWN HARBOR

Scale 8000.

0 5 10 20 40 60 rods

101

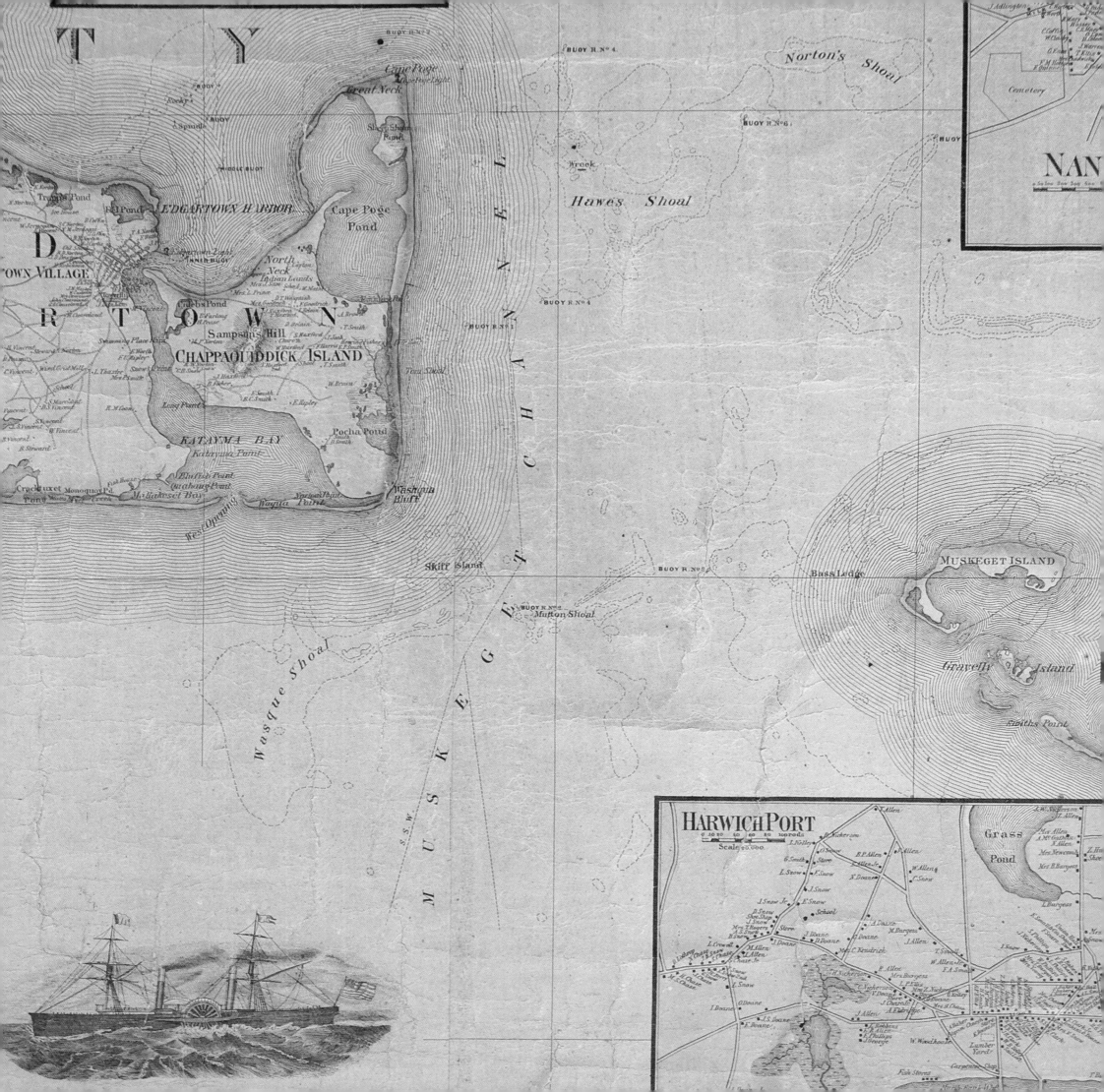

Nantucket County

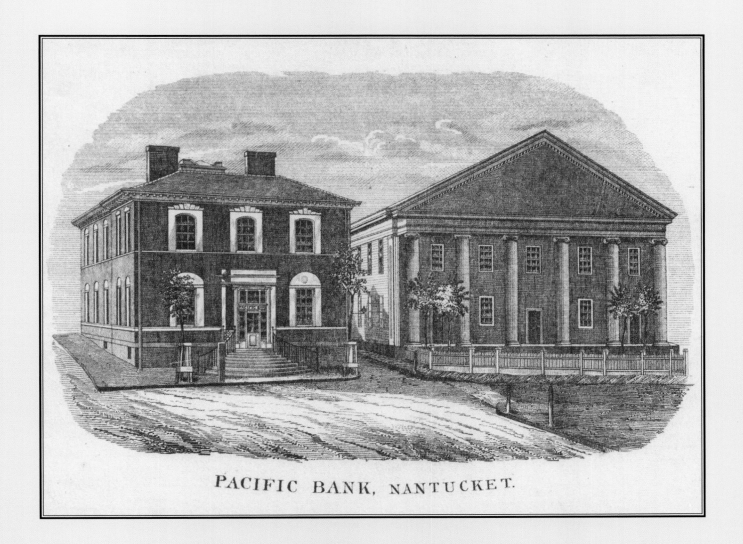

PACIFIC BANK, NANTUCKET.

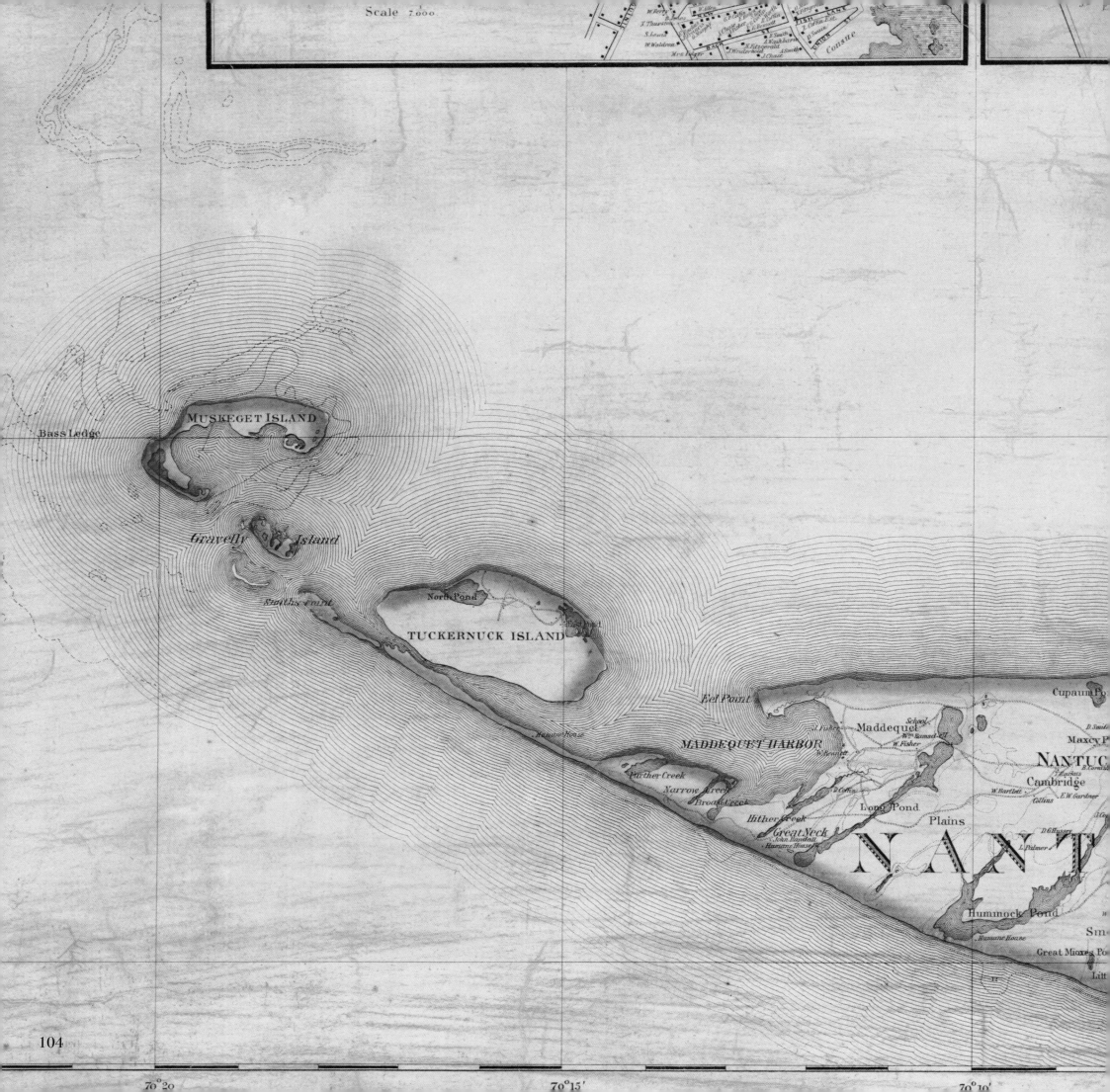

Bass Ledge

MUSKEGET ISLAND

Gravelly Island

Smith Point

North Pond

TUCKERNUCK ISLAND

East Pond

Eel Point

Humane House

MADDEQUET HARBOR

J. Fisher

Wm. Ramsdell

Maddequet

W. Fisher

School

W. Bennett

Cupaum Po

D. Smith

Maxcy P

NANTUC

Cambridge

B. Cornish

W. Bartlett

Collins

E.W. Gardner

Prather Creek

Narrow Creek

Broad Creek

D. Coffin

Long Pond

Plains

D.G. Hussey

Hither Creek

L. Palmer

Great Neck
John Randall
Humane House

N A N T

Hummock Pond

Humane House

Sm

Great Mioxes Po

Litt

Great Point

Great Point Light
J.B. Nicholson

Humane House

Croskaty Pond
P.H.Folger

Humane House

Head
of the Harbor

Shoal Spots
discovered in 1847

10 feet Shoal
discovered in
1848

41°20'

Pocomo Head

Pocomo
J.E.Eldridge

Squam
Squam
T.Ray

Coatue Beach

COATUE BEACH

Polpis Harbor

Quaise

POLPIS

Sechacha Pond

Septenian House

Outer Bars
Cliff Shoal
Whale Rock
Buo Lights

Coatue Flats

Coatue Point

Shimo Point

Shawaukemo

Sechacha

Sankaty Light
A.B.Bunker
Sankaty Head

NANTUCKET
HARBOR

Autshimeo

Middle Pasture

Plainfield

VILLAGE

North Pasture

Gibbs Pond

Gibbs
Swamp

CKET COUNTY

Bloomingdale

Patrick's Rip Shoal

Bass's Rip Shoal

South Pasture

SIASCONSET

South East Quarter

41°15'

Miacomet Pond
Pond

Weedweeder Ponds

Nobadeer Pond

Madequecham Pond

Toochki Pond

Pocha Pond

Tom Nevers Head

Humane House

105

Weetweeder Shoal

70°05'   70°00'   69°55'

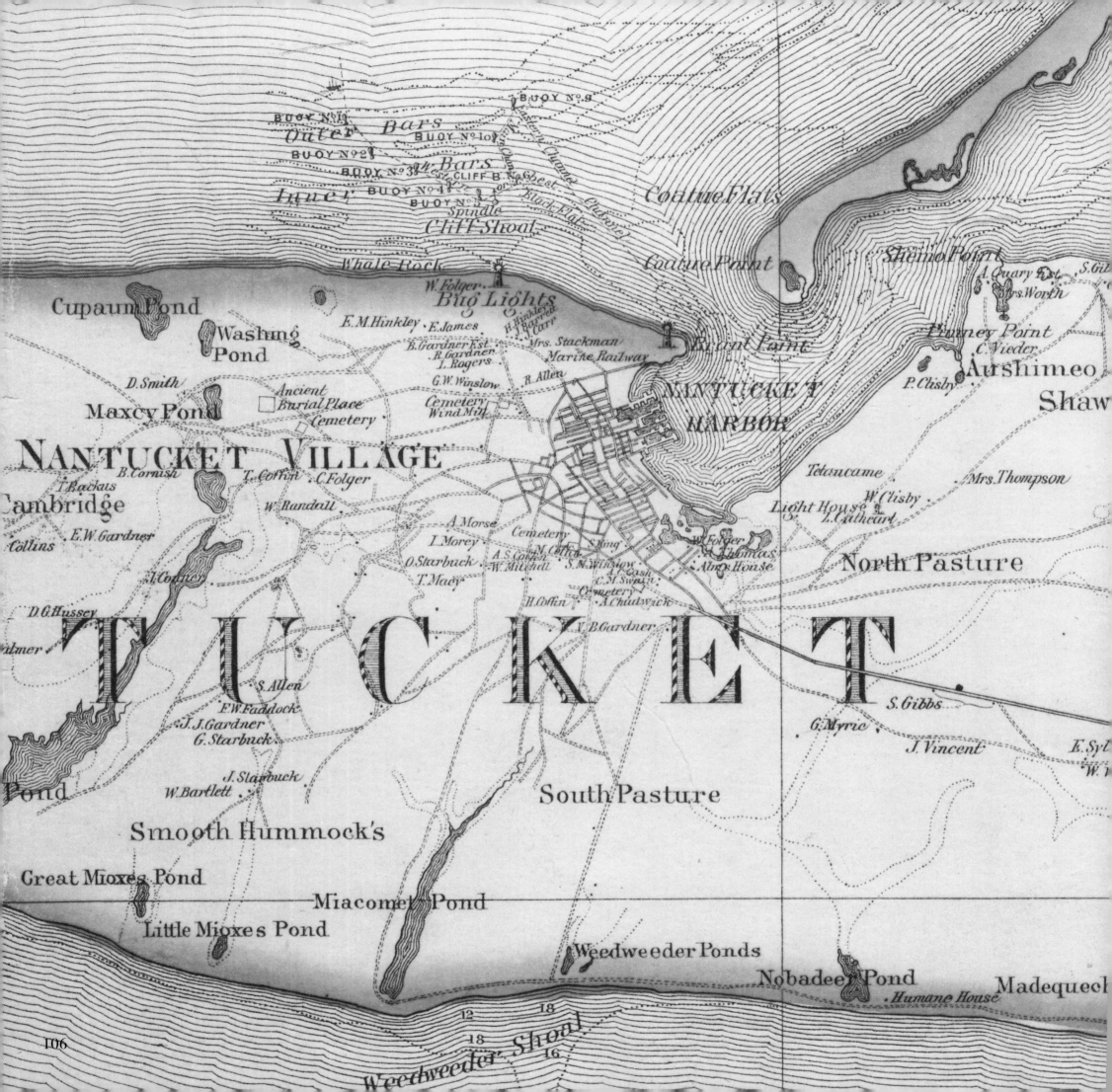

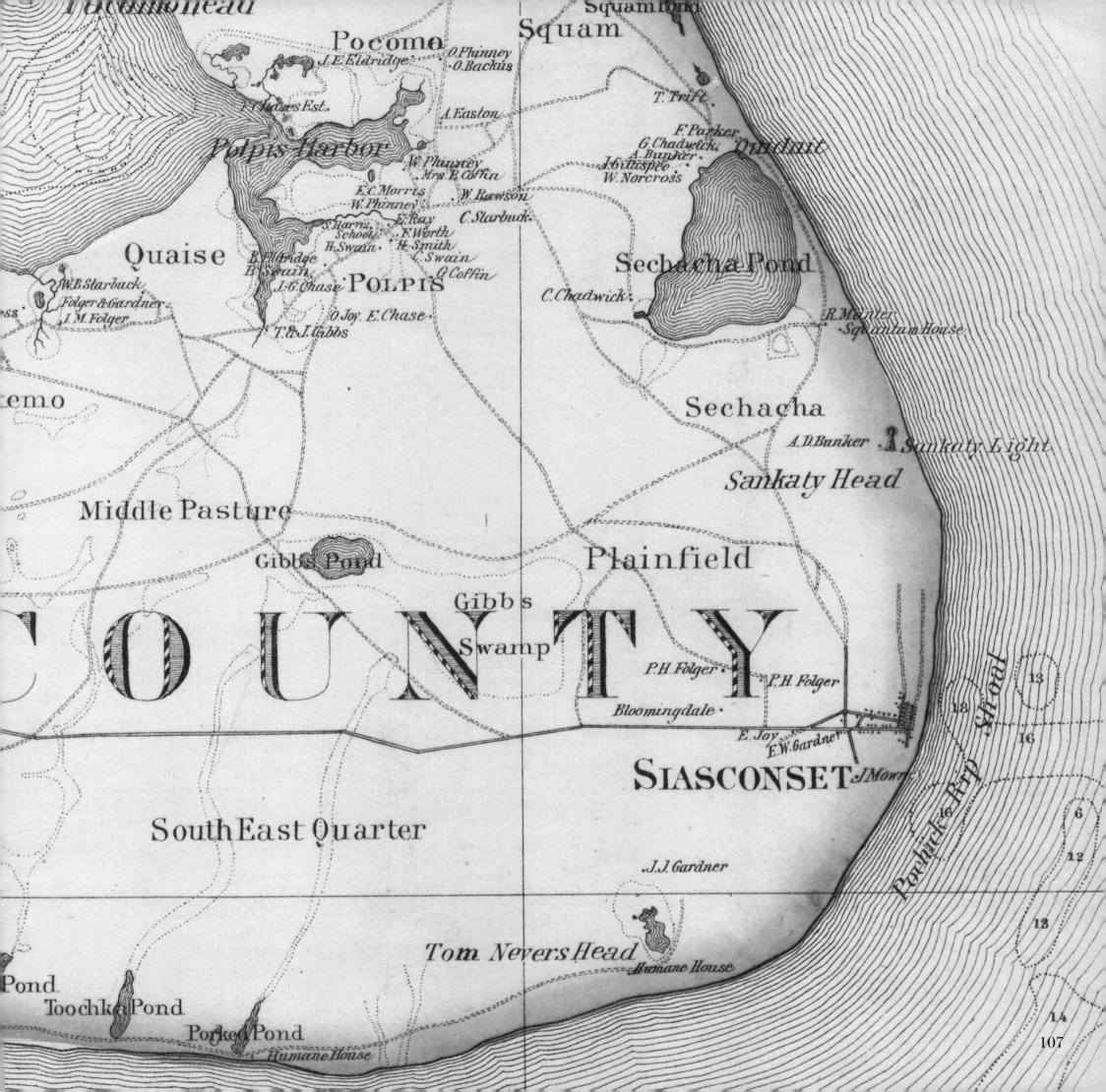

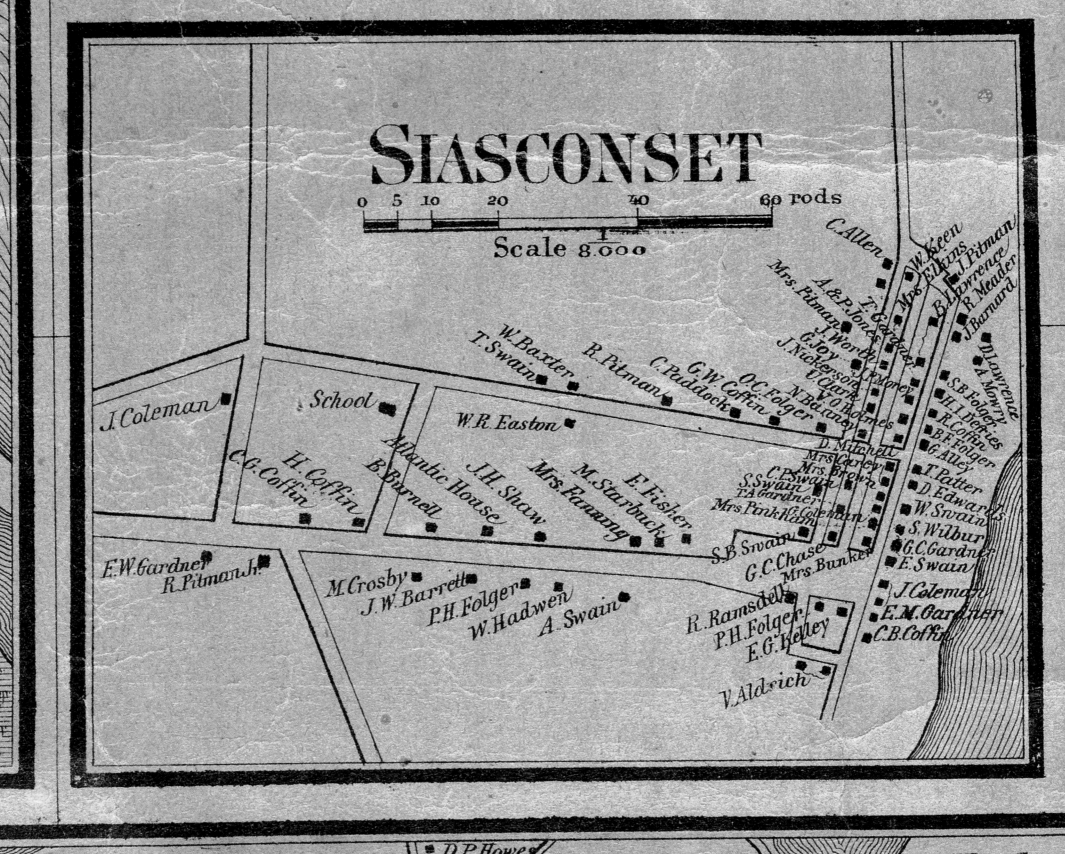

SIASCONSET

0 5 10 20 40 60 rods

Scale 8.000

C. Allen

W. Keen
Mrs Elkins
J. Pitman
A. & P. Jones
T. Gardner
B. Lawrence
R. Meader
Mrs. Pitman
J. Worth
J. Barnard
G. Joy
J. Morey
J. Nickerson
D. Lawrence
N. Barney
A. Mowry
J. Clark
V. O. Holmes
S. B. Folger
O. C. Folger
H. L. Defries
G. W. Coffin
R. Coffin
C. Paddock
B. F. Folger
R. Pitman
G. Alley
W. Baxter
T. Patter
T. Swain
D. Mitchell
D. Edwards
Mrs Carey
Mrs Brown
W. R. Easton
C. P. Swain
W. Swain
F. Fisher
S. Swain
S. Wilbur
M. Starbuck
T. A. Gardner
G. C. Gardner
J. Coleman
Mrs Fanning
Mrs Pinkham
G. Coleman
E. Swain
School
J. H. Shaw
H. Coffin
S. B. Swain
C. G. Coffin
B. Burnell
Atlantic House
G. C. Chase
Mrs. Bunker
J. Coleman
E. W. Gardner
R. Ramsdell
E. M. Gardner
R. Pitman Jr.
P. H. Folger
C. B. Coffin
M. Crosby
E. G. Kelley
J. W. Barrett
P. H. Folger
W. Hadwen
A. Swain
V. Aldrich

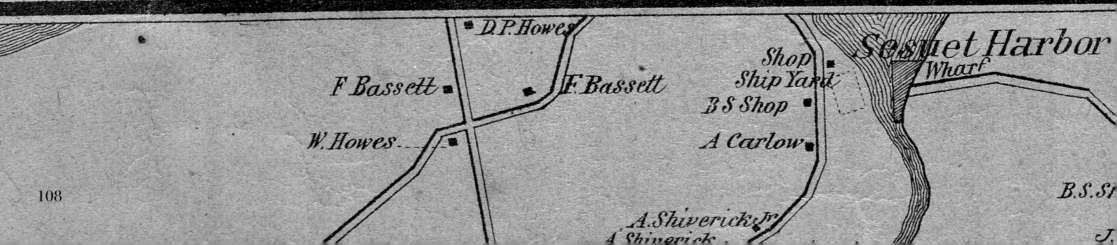

D. P. Howes

Sesuet Harbor

Shop
Ship Yard
Wharf

F. Bassett

F. Bassett

B S Shop

W. Howes

A Carlow

108

A. Shiverick Jr.
A. Shiverick

B. S. St

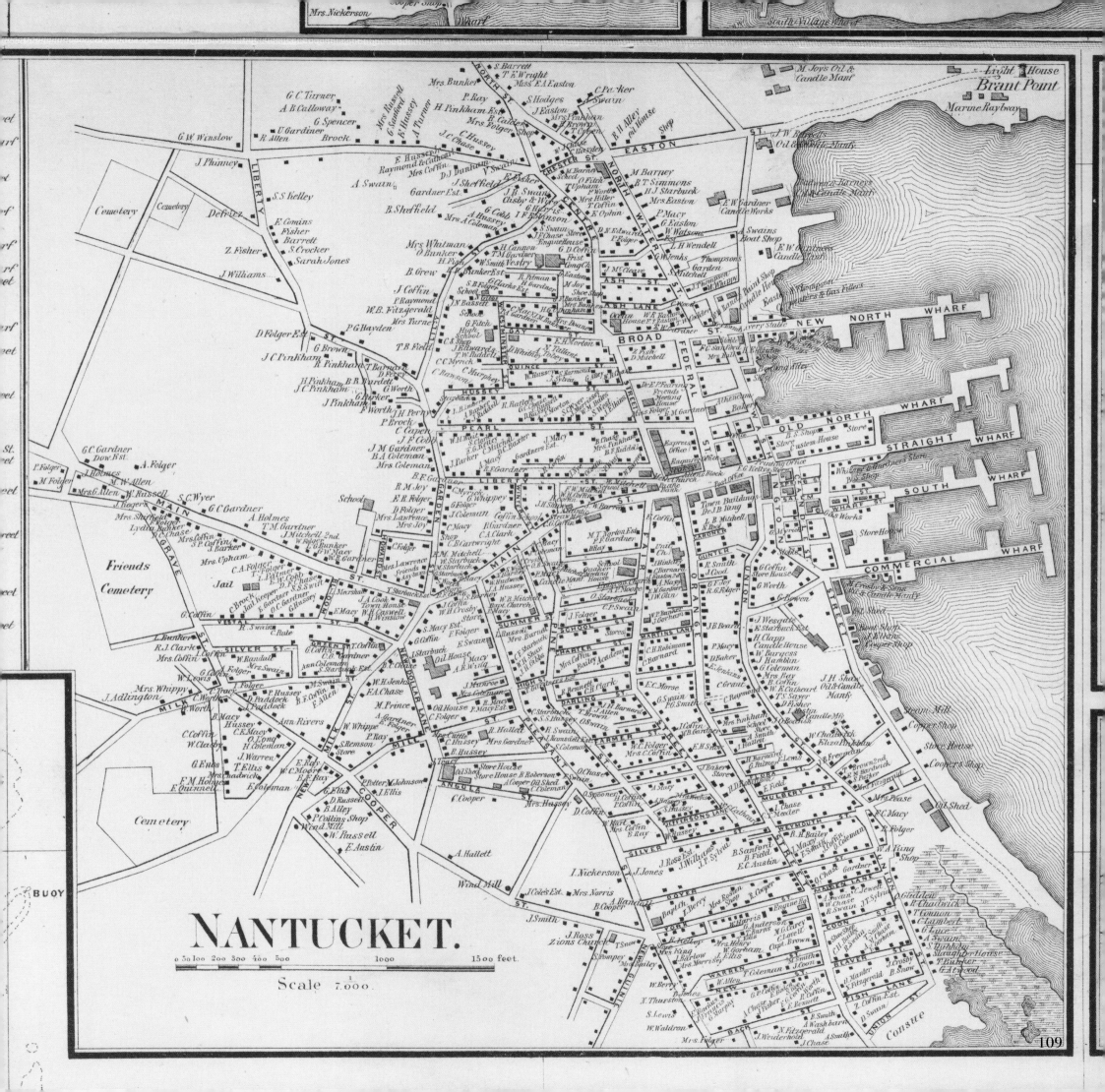

NANTUCKET.

Scale $\frac{1}{7.000}$

0 50 100 200 300 400 500   1000   1500 feet.

Brant Point

Light House

109

110

G. C. Turner
A. B. Calloway
G. Spencer
G. W. Winslow
R. Allen
U. Gardner
Brock

Mrs. Bunker
Mrs. Russell
G. Sanford
F. Hussey
A. Turner
P. Ray
H. Pinkham Est.
Mrs. Folger Shop
R. Calder
J. C. Chase
C. Hussey

NORTH ST.
S. Barrett
T. E. Wright
Miss E.A.Ea
S. Hodge
J. Easto
CHE

J. Phinney
LIBERTY
S. S. Kelley
Defriez
E. Comins
Fisher
Barrett
S. Crocker
Sarah Jones
Z. Fisher
J. Williams

E. Hussey Jr.
Raymond & Cathcart
Mrs. Coffin
A. Swain
Gardner Est.
D. J. Dunham
V. Swa
J. Sheffield
B. Sheffield
Mrs. A. Coleman
A. Hussey
G. Cobb
Mrs. Whitman
O. Bunker
H. Fish
B. Grew
E. B. Bunker Est.

E. Fisher
J. B. Swain
Clisby & Wife
G. Harris
I. F. Robinso
J. F. Chas
Engine
H. Cannon
T. M. Gardner
W. Smith Vestry

D. Folger Est.
ST.
P. G. Hayden
G. Brown
J. C. Pinkham
R. Pinkham
T. Barnard
D. Ferry
H. Pinkham
B. R. Burdett
J. C. Pinkham
G. Worth
J. Pinkham
G. Parker
F. Worth
J. H. Perry
P. Brock
C. Capen
J. F. Cobb

J. Coffin
P. Raymond
W. B. Fitzgerald
Mrs. Turner
T. B. Field

School
S. B. Folger
J. N. Bassett
N. Gibbs
School
G. Fitch
High
School
C. S. Shop
J. Edwards
T. W. Riddell
C. C. Myrick
C. Rawson

R. Pitman
H. Gardner
G. Clarks Est.
A. Gardner
C. Macy
J. M. Buk
N. Tob
D. Whitney
A. C
C. Murphey
W. Hussey
J. S

WESTMINSTER ST.
GAY
QUINCE

HUSSEY
Starbuck
I. B. Imber
A. Bunker
J. Riddell
R. Ratler
G. C. Chase
D. H. Russell
J. Mo

PEARL

W. H. Wait
S. Clark
E. G. Kelley
C. Mitchell
D. C. Baxter
J. Parker
A. Macy
Gardners Est.
R. F. Gardner
J. M
M

G. C. Gardner
Dow Est.
A. Folger
P. Folger
J. Holmes
M. Folger
M. W. Allen
Mrs. G. Allen
W. Russell
S. C. Wyer
J. Rogers
G. C. Gardner
Mrs. Sheffield
A. Holmes
F. Folger
T. M. Gardner
Lydia Bunker
D. C. Chase
Mrs. Coffin
S. P. Coffin
J. Barker
Mrs. Upham
J. Mitchell 2nd.
W. Folger
L. G. Bunker
G. W. Macy
W. R. Gardner
C. A. Folger
T. Folger
L. Palmer
E. W. Cobb
D. F. Chase
S. S. Swift
C. Brock
Jail Keeper
E. Gardner
O. C. Gardner
G. Hussey

J. M. Gardner
B. A. Coleman
Mrs. Coleman
B. F. Gardner
R. M. Joy
E. R. Folger
D. Folger
Mrs. Lawrence
Mrs. Joy

C. Myrick
G. Whippey
G. Folger
J. Coleman
C. Macy
Shop
C. B. Cartwright

LIBERTY
WINTER
J. H. Sh
R
Coffin School
E. Gardner
C. A. Clark
C. C. G

School
C. Folger
Mrs. Lawrence
Friends
Asylum
E. M. Mitchell
W. Starbuck
M. Starbuck
G. Starbuck
S. Worth
Store
T. Starbuck Est.
L. Marshall
J. A. Cook
Town House
W. H. Caswell
H. Winslow
B. F. Coffin
J. S. Barney
W. B. Mitchell
Bapt. Church
Store

MAIN
MATN
S. Wilber
N. Barney
J. A. Hussey
J. Coffin
W. H. Crosby
O. B. Swai
T. Macy
E. Macy
P. Mac
Can
SUMMER ST.
O. B. Sw

HOWARD ST.
GARDEN
BLOOM

Friends
Cemetery
Jail
GRAVE ST.

G. Coffin
VESTAL
R. Swain
C. Rule
L. Bunker
R. J. Clark
C. Russell
Mrs. Barnet
E. Swain
GREEN ST.
T. Coffin
G. Coffin
F. Folger
L. Russell
back

M. Joys Oil & Candle Manf

Light House
Brant Point

Marine Raybway

C. Parker Swain

E H Alley oil House

Shop

EASTON ST.

J W Barretts Oil & Candle Manf

M Barney
R T Simmons
H J Starbuck
Mrs Easton
E W Gardner Candle Works

P. Macy
G. Easton
W. Watsons Est

NORTH WATER

D N Edwards
P Folger

L H Wendell
G W Jenks

A Swains Boat Shop

E W Gardners Candle Manf

Gadwen & Barneys Candle Manf

J McCleave

S. Mitchell
Thompson's Garden
J. Thompson
W. Whippy

ASH ST.

ASH LANE

C. Wood

Easton & Thompson Carpenters & Gas Filters

Ocean House

W R Easton
F F Easton
T W Colder

W R Bands Paint Shop
Candle House

E W Gardner

BROAD ST.

Mrs Rand Livery Stable

NEW   NORTH   WHARF

Z Fish
D Mitchell

Stable
F C Sanford
Mrs Ball

B Ellingdale

FEDERAL

Dr E P Fearing
Friends Meeting House
Miss Folger
E M Gardner

Athenæum
Baker

Bowling Alley

Shop

WASH

OLD   NORTH   WHARF

STREET

B. Chase
Mrs. Pinkham
B. F. Riddell

Express Office

Enquirer Office
STORES
Athens Block

Printing Office
E G Kelly's Store

B. S. Shops
Store

Store

Custom House

Whitney & Harpers Store

WHARF

STRAIGHT   WHARF

Dr Church
Pacific Bank

Post Office

SPRING ST.

B. Shop

WHARF

W Barney

Town Buildings
Dr J B King
L B Mitchell
N Pool

GARDNER

G. Myrick

SALEM

WHARF ST.

Gas Works

SOUTH

Store House

WHARF

M T Norton Est
F F Gardner

F. Coffin

GUNTER

UNION

Store House

Unit Ch.

J Hinkley
C Barnard
J Easton 2d
A. Macy
E M Gardner
J W Olin

R. Smith
J. Cood

ORANGE

G Coffin Store House
G F Joy
R G Folger

G. Worth

G. Bowen

Stable

COMMERCIAL

H. Crosby & Sons Oil & Candle Manf

Episcop. Church
A P Moore
O. Starbuck
C P Swain

W P Bunker
J Gorham

MARTINS LANE

J. Wesgate
E. Starbuck Est
H. Clapp

J B Beard

STREET

Oil Shed

Boat Shop

SOUTH
WES

0   10   20   40

Pawhun

R B

F Ba

J E Baker
F. Baker
M. Baker

Cemetery
Bap Church

B. Berry

A. Berry
A. Robbins
Mathews & Co
E. Barker
W. Oliver

School
D & B Mathews

J. Baker
Polly Sherman
B. Crowell

A

W. Teter
A Lewis
I. Studdey
J. F. Mathews

Mrs Bassett

I. Sherman
Mrs Bake
B. Ma

J. Baker
Mathews
E. Parker
Shop

Mrs Crowell

Mrs Howes

111

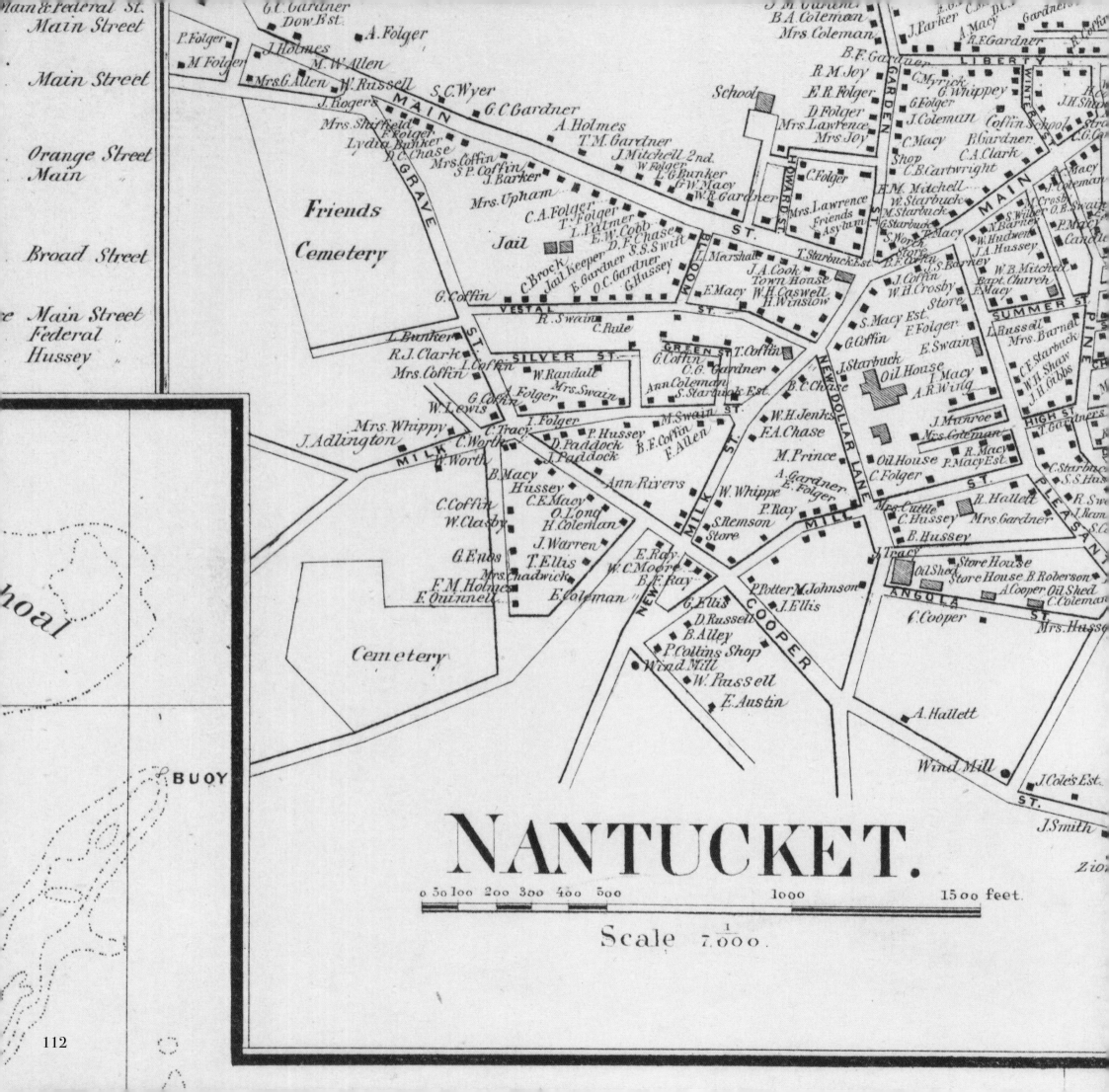

NANTUCKET.

Scale $\frac{1}{7,000}$

0 30 100 200 300 400 500   1000   1500 feet.

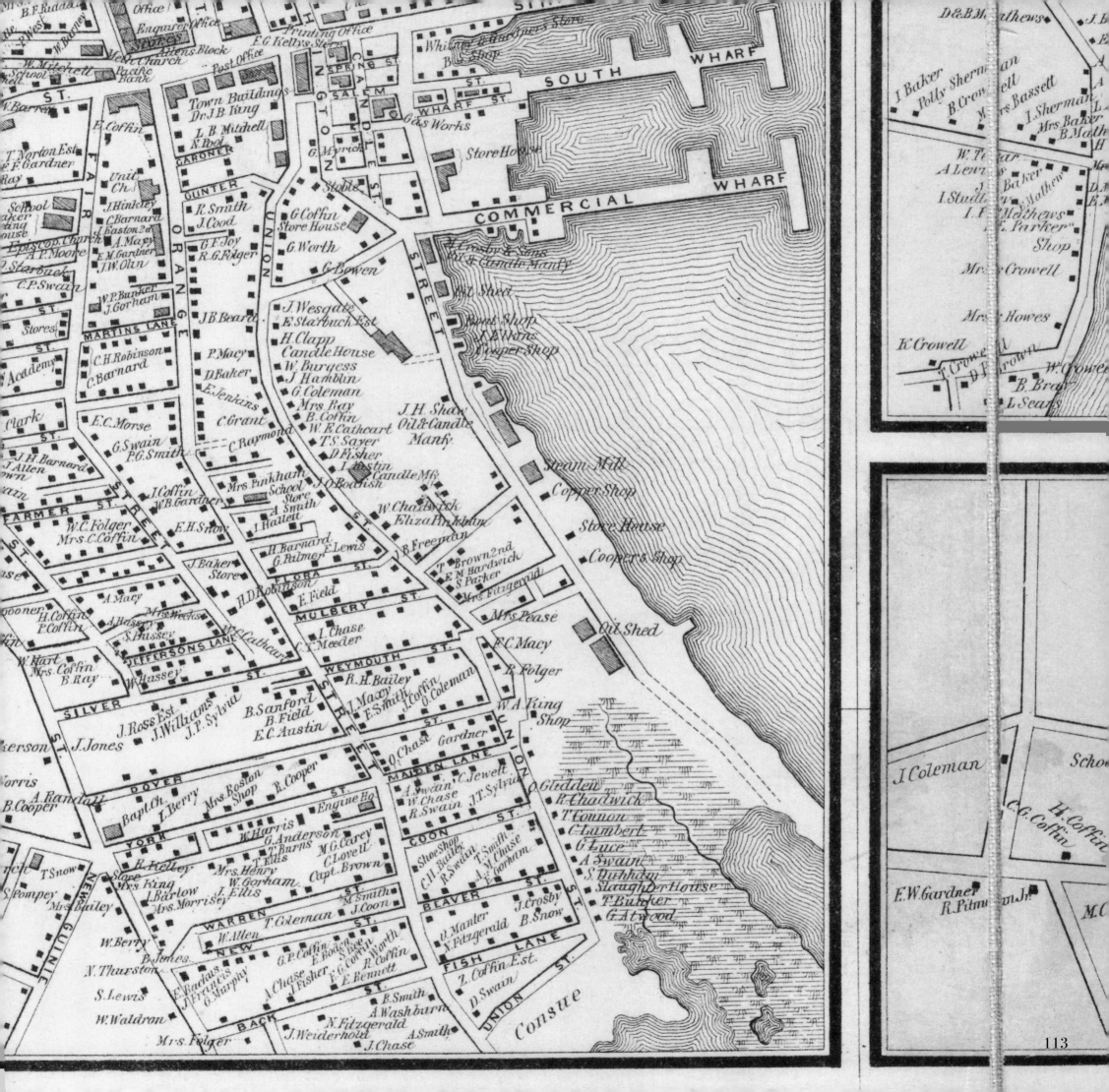

BUSINESS DIRECTORY.

BANKS & INSURANCE COMPANIES.

Pacific Bank, Main Street
J. W. Barrett Prest Wm Mitchell Cashr F. M. Mitchell Asst Cashr
Savings Institution, Main Street Wm Mitchell Treasr
Commercial Insurance Comp.
F. M. Mitchell Prest A. J. Morton Secry.
T. A. Gardner, Underwriters Agent   Main Street

IMPORTERS OF SPERM OIL.

G. & M. Starbuck & Co.   Main Street
L. & P. Macy,
E. W. Perry.   Cross Wharf

OIL & CANDLE MANFR'S.

J. W. Barrett & Co.
Hadwen & Barney,
J. H. Shaw
M. Crosby & Son,
M. Joy,

SHIP CHANDLERS & COMMISSION MERCHTS.

Whitney & Gardner,   Straight Wharf
J. B. Macy,
E. G. Kelley,   Exchange Building "
G. W. Macy,   Main Street
T. A. Gardner

GROCERY & PROVISION DEALERS.

T. W. Calder,   Main Street
B. C. Chase,
N. Tallant,   Cross Wharf
N. Fitzgerald,   Fair Street

DRY GOODS & CLOTHING DEALERS.

Bates Cook & Co.   Main Street
Bovey & Coffin,
E. H. Alley & Co.

HARDWARE DEALERS

G. W. Macy,   Main Street
J. G. Tuck,   " "

DEALERS IN WATCHES & JEWELRY.

Hammond & Co   Kelley's Block

LIBRARIES & READING ROOMS.

Nantucket Atheneum,   Federal Street
Commercial News Room   Main "
Exchange Room   " "
Pacific Room   " "

Chas H. Eggar, Drugs & Fancy Goods   Centre Street
E. Mitchell, Books   Main "
Robinson & Macy, Lumber Dealers   South Wharf
E. W. Perry, Grain & Coal Dealer   Cross "
T. W. Riddell, Auctioneer   Straight "
C. H. Bailey, Union Store   Main Street
C. H. Robinson, Marble Worker   Fair "
Easton & Thompson, Carpenters & Gas Fitters   Broad "
Fisher & Bodfish, Carpenters   Old North Wharf
S. Hodges, Ship Carpenter.   North "
A. Swain, Boat Builder.
A. Smith, Blacksmith   New North Wharf
E. Smith, Supt Marine Railway
J. Parker, Wood Merchant   Cross Wharf
J. Elkins, Cooper   Washington Street
W. H. Coffin Painter
W. B. Rand, House & Sign Painter,   Broad "
Chase & Cook, Bakers   Lower Pearl
R. Ratleff, Rigger   South Wharf
C. Raymond, Caulker
W. Summerhays, Artist   Centre Street
W. C. Folger, Surveyor   Fair "

PHYSICIANS.

Dr. E. P. Fearing.   Centre Street
"   C. F. Robinson,
"   J. B. King   Union "

PRINTERS.

Morissey & Moore, Publishers of Inquirer   Corner Main & Federal St.
Hussey & Robinson, Publishers of Mirror   Main Street

COLLECTOR OF CUSTOMS.

E. W. Allen,   Main Street
C. P. Swain, Post Master

LAWYERS.

E. M. Gardner,   Orange Street
J. M. Bunker,   Main "
A. G. Bunker, Register of Deeds
Geo. Cobb, Clerk of Courts

Ocean House, Jervis Robinson Proprietor   Broad Street

T. Brown, 2nd Master, Steamer Island Home
A. B. Robinson, Agt. for N. & C.C. Steam Boat Co. Office   Main Street
Colemans Express.   Federal "
C. Murphey, Bill Poster & Town Crier,   Hussey "

Contributors and Acknowledgments

Resid of S.B.Phinney Esq. Custom House School Ho. Unit Church

VIEW IN MAIN STREET BARNSTABLE.

Contributors

Robert Finch is an award-winning nature writer and editor. Mr. Finch is the author of many books including *The Primal Place, Common Ground: A Naturalist's Cape Cod, Death of a Hornet and Other Cape Cod Essays, Outlands: Journeys to the Outer Edges of Cape Cod, Special Places on Cape Cod and the Islands*, and *The Iambics of Newfoundland: Notes from an Unknown Shore*. He is editor of *A Place Apart: A Cape Cod Reader* and coeditor (with John Elder) of *Nature Writing: The Tradition in English*. Mr. Finch is also an award-winning weekly contributor to WCAI, The Cape and Islands NPR station.

Theresa Mitchell Barbo of Yarmouth Port is a writer of historical nonfiction. Her books are published by The History Press and include *The Cape Cod Murder of 1899, True Accounts of Yankee Ingenuity & Grit, The Pendleton Disaster off Cape Cod: The Greatest Small Boat Rescue in Coast Guard History*, second edition [on the Commandant's recommended reading list for leadership], *Cape Cod Bay: A History of Salt & Sea*, and *Nantucket Sound: A Maritime History*. She presents illustrated lectures to listening audiences. Ms. Barbo is founder of the annual Cape Cod Maritime History Symposium, partnered with the Cape Cod Museum of Natural History. She holds BA and MA degrees from the University of Massachusetts Dartmouth and has studied executive integral leadership at the University of Notre Dame.

Elliott Carr moved from the Boston area to Cape Cod twenty-seven years ago. As a Cape banking and community leader, he has always tried to balance economic and environmental issues, believing maintenance of the Cape's attractive landscape is equally important to business and economic interests and the quality of life. In 1995, Carr walked the entire shoreline of Cape Cod, swimming thirty-three channels and embayments. In 1997, he wrote *Walking the Shores of Cape Cod* about that adventure and his observations concerning a wide variety of Cape Cod shoreline issues. During the past fourteen years, he has written columns for the *Cape Codder*, the *Cape Cod Times*, and the *Cape Cod Voice*.

Jim Coogan is a well-known Cape Cod historian and lecturer. Together with Jack Sheedy, Mr. Coogan has coauthored three books about the Cape: *Cape Cod Companion: The History and Mystery of Old Cape Cod, Cape Cod Voyage: A Journey Through Cape Cod's History and Lore*, and *Cape Cod Harvest: A Gathering in of Cape Cod Stories*. His book *Sail Away Ladies: Stories of Cape Cod Women in the Age of Sail* won the 2004 US Maritime Literature Award. He is a regular columnist for the *Cape Cod Times* daily newspaper and a frequent contributor to area publications.

Charles Fields majored in photography at Paier College of Art in Hamden, Connecticut. For the past three decades, Mr. Fields has continued to perfect both his photographic eye and technique. Adept at traditional and digital imaging, he has established himself as one of New England's foremost photographers. In 2000, he founded Fields Publishing, an award-winning publisher of fine art and photography books and calendars. (Visit www.charlesfields.net to learn more about what's happening at Fields Publishing.) He is currently publishing a photographic book featuring Nantucket Island. For the past several years, he has been working on a Vietnam photo book as well as conducting photography workshops and tours in Vietnam.

Gail Fields, painter and graphic design artist, graduated from Parson's School of Design in New York City. She is a commissioned artist, with three of her works now part of the US Coast Guard permanent collection in Washington, DC. An award-winning artist, Ms. Fields is currently devoting her time to painting in her studio in Provincetown, Massachussetts. Most recently, she was invited to exhibit her paintings, GardenScapes & Landscapes at the Cape Cod Museum of Art in Dennis, Massachussetts. Her work can be seen at www.gailfields-artist.com. As a graphic designer with Fields Publishing, she was part of the production team that was awarded the Benjamin Franklin winner for Best Art Book (2007) and finalist for Best Coffee Table Book (2009).

Adam Gamble serves as publisher at On Cape Publications, Inc., and Our World of Books, LLC. He is the author of *In the Footsteps of Thoreau*, coauthor (with Takesato Watanabe) of *A Public Betrayed*, and the editor of the *1880 Atlas of Barnstable County*. He conceived of, designed, and wrote most of the more than forty titles in the Good Night Our World series of board books for preschoolers, including *Good Night Cape Cod* and *Good Night World*. The series has sold more than one million copies.

Dr. Joseph Garver is the reference librarian of the Harvard Map Collection of the Harvard College Library. He has been the interim head of the collection since 2008. He served for ten years as the editor of the Boston Map Society Newsletter. Having curated numerous map exhibits, with a particular focus on historical cartography of New England, he is also the author of the acclaimed book *Surveying the Shore: Historic Maps of Coastal Massachusetts, 1600–1930*. Dr. Garver is currently working on a book on the historical cartography of Rhode Island. Visit the amazing Harvard Map Collection online at http://hcl.harvard.edu/libraries/maps/.

Dr. Kathleen Schatzberg has served as president of Cape Cod Community College since 1998. She is a member of many boards of organizations on the Cape and Islands as well as national organizations. Her career includes thirty-five years as an administrator and faculty member at various colleges, as well as earlier positions as a high-school teacher of English and in business. Her passion for community colleges is rooted in their role as cultural centers for their communities, as well as their commitment to social justice in providing opportunity to those who might otherwise not have it. As an avid reader and a community-college administrator, she can happily delve into almost any academic field, including, of course, history.

Acknowledgments

Kathleen Schatzberg and Elliott Carr, in addition to writing their essays, have been instrumental in supporting and encouraging this publication.

Natalie DuBois, Executive Director of the Cape Cod Community College Educational Foundation, Inc., and Gerry Desautels, Foundation Development Associate, were exceedingly helpful in getting this project off the ground. Mr. Desautels has been a great asset. He dedicated many hours to supporting virtually every aspect of the project.

Thanks to Allen Wannamaker and Gordon Wright at Cape Cod Five for supporting this book and providing valuable comments and insights along the way. Their enthusiasm helped move this book from theory to reality.

Charles Fields generously volunteered to photograph the 1858 *Map of the Counties of Barnstable, Dukes and Nantucket, Massachusetts* owned by Cape Cod Community College. Charles also worked with his wife, Gail Fields, to help design this book.

Jeanmarie L. Fraser, Associate Dean of Learning Resources at the college, and Georgia Carvalho, College Grants Developer, were also supportive throughout.

Mary Sicchio, Archivist at the William Brewster Nickerson Cape Cod History Archives, has supported this project continuously. In fact, the idea of publishing the map in book form was her idea.

James Warren, staff artist at the *Cape Cod Times* and a faculty member at Cape Cod Community College, offered critical technical contributions to the design.

This book was copy edited by Susan Bouse of Bouse Editorial in Denver, Colorado. Thanks to Ms. Bouse for going the extra mile. She made many useful suggestions on the design and content.

Editor Stuard M. Derrick also reviewed this book, providing many helpful suggestions.

Thanks also to the William Brewster Nickerson Cape Cod History Archives Advisory Committee and Campaign Steering Committee for all of their support of the archives and of this book. Joshua "Jan" A. Nickerson Jr. is the Honorary Chairperson. The Advisory Committee includes: Adam Gamble, Elliott Carr, Joshua "Jan" A. Nickerson Jr., Nathaniel Philbrick, Patricia A. Cahill, Robert Finch, Sally Gunning, Theresa Mitchell Barbo, Daniel J. Lombardo, and Joan Bentinck-Smith. The Campaign Steering Committee includes: Ann M. Williams, Adelaide Queeney, David Willard, Jim Coogan, John W. Miller, Kathleen Schatzberg, Laura Flanders, Michael J. Miller, Richard G. Rand, and Holbrook R. Davis.

Special thanks to Sung Yun of Sung In America, Inc., for providing superior printing services.

Index

BARNSTABLE BANK YARMOUTH PORT.

Index

HARBOR OF PROVINCETOWN 1620.